THE
PERFECT
PRESENTATION

JOAN MINNINGER, Ph.D., and
BARBARA GOULTER

THE PERFECT PRESENTATION

DOUBLEDAY

New York   Toronto   London   Sydney   Auckland

PUBLISHED BY DOUBLEDAY

a division of Bantam Doubleday Dell Publishing Group, Inc.
666 Fifth Avenue, New York, New York 10103

DOUBLEDAY and the portrayal of an anchor with a dolphin
are trademarks of Doubleday,
a division of Bantam Doubleday Dell Publishing Group, Inc.

LIBRARY OF CONGRESS-CATALOGING-IN-PUBLICATION DATA

Minninger, Joan.
The perfect presentation / Joan Minninger and Barbara Goulter.—
1st ed.
p.   cm.
1. Business presentations.   2. Public speaking.   I. Goulter,
Barbara.   II. Title
HF5718.22.M56   1991
658.4'52—dc20   91-6656
                                                        CIP

ISBN 0-385-41543-5

Book design and title page art by Patrice Fodero

Illustration by Jackie Aher

To Bob Goulding
a perfect presenter
great teacher, great friend

To Vic
a believer

ACKNOWLEDGMENTS

Special gratitude to the Commonwealth Club for their kind permission to print "The Corporation Without Boundaries," presented by Robert Haas on December 1, 1989; also to all our clients, who influenced us at least as much as we influenced them; to Eleanor Knowles Dugan and Becky Gordon for editorial assistance; to Sandra Schrift, Janelle Barlow, Patricia Fripp and Barbara Sanner for their continuing support; to all our friends at the National Speakers Association; and to Michael Larsen and John Duff, agent and editor, always a pleasure to work with.

CONTENTS

THE
PERFECT
PRESENTATION

HOW TO USE THIS BOOK

*T*here are many books on presentation skills and public speaking. Can this one be any different?

It can be, and is.

Some years ago, I left university teaching to give communication seminars for corporations. At the same time, I went into private practice as a psychotherapist, helping people get through speaking and writing blocks. Most speech books emphasize one aspect or the other. *The Perfect Presentation* deals with both.

The Perfect Presentation features a *process*—a step-by-step guide that will unblock you where you are blocked and free you to achieve your highest professional level of presentation skills. It also features many true stories, taken mainly from my own practice, demonstrating how others have achieved the same high performance.

You will be guided through this process by flowcharts, based on a simple yet comprehensive view of the elements that go into a successful presentation. You can trust this process because it has worked for thousands.

There are three elements to every presentation:

The speaker (yourself)
The listeners (your audience)
The content (your prepared speech, your materials)

All three must be in harmony for a presentation to succeed. Dull speakers alienate their listeners, no matter how good their material may be.

Enthusiastic speakers and fine material are wasted on an unsuitable audience. And nothing can make up for a pointless, meandering, inaccurate content.

But when all three are right, there's no way a presentation can fail. It all adds up, as simple as second-grade arithmetic:

> **A ready speaker**
> **+ an appropriate audience**
> **+ well-organized materials**
> —————————————————
> **A Perfect Presentation**

My* process gives you a way of putting them together. I like to think of it in terms of track and field:

Ready (yourself)
On Your Mark (with your audience)
Get Set (with your materials)
Go—and give a perfect presentation

This track-and-field model fits neatly into the accompanying simple flowchart, which I call the *Primary Flowchart*. This Primary Flowchart

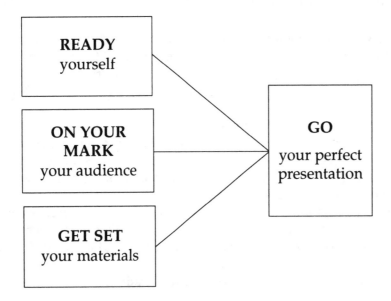

serves two purposes. First, it makes the process clear and plain. Second, it suggests the right questions. **Just how do you "ready yourself"? Or get "on the mark" with your audience? Or "get set" with your materials?**

*Although this book is a collaboration, the words *my* and *I* will always refer to Joan Minninger and her personal experiences with clients or professional speaking.

Let's begin at the beginning. How do you "ready yourself"? What are the steps involved?

First, you need to ready your *head*. That is, you need to:

1. define your subject, and
2. master it.

At the same time, though perhaps not quite so obviously, you need to ready your *heart*. That is, you need to:

1. move through stage fright,
2. clarify your agendas, and
3. develop an enthusiastic attitude and manner.

If a presentation is to succeed, a ready heart and a ready head are equally essential. As a speaker, you need something valuable to say. But you also need the capacity to stand up in front of other people and say it effectively.

This process of readying head and heart can also be summed up, as in the following flowchart, which allows you to see the whole process in a single glance. Charts like these will guide you all the way through

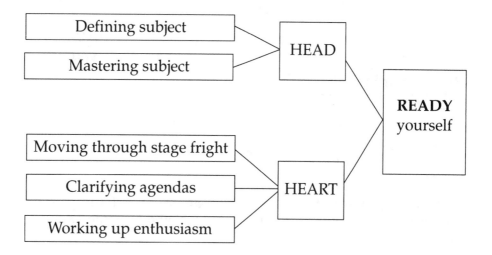

The Perfect Presentation. You will find them amazingly useful. They will help you to keep track, at all times, of exactly where in the process you are.

Each time we begin one of the three major topics, the *Primary Flowchart* will be there for you, highlighted appropriately. For example, we will start the *Get Ready* chapter with the following chart:

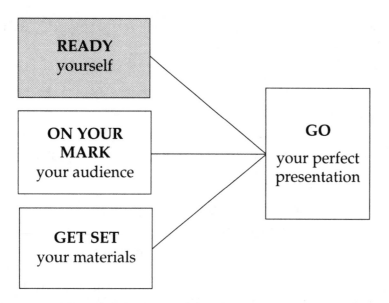

Then, as we move from one subtopic to another, you will find a *Secondary Flowchart*, also highlighted. For example, when we take up *Moving Through Stage Fright*, the section will begin with this:

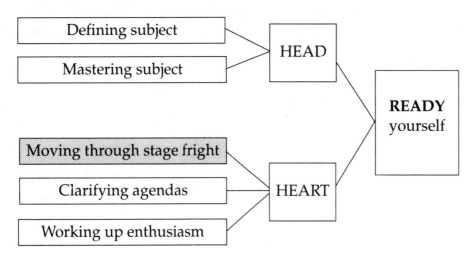

And when we finish with *Moving Through Stage Fright* and go on to *Clarifying Agendas*, you will find that topic highlighted, as the next chart shows.

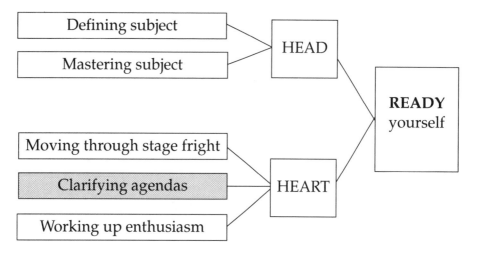

You will see instantly where you have been, where you are, and where you are going. You will see how each aspect contributes, how everything fits.

As you move on to the later stages, you will discover how to tailor your presentations to the needs of different audiences, how to organize, compose, and remember your materials, and how to present them with ease and effectiveness.

The Perfect Presentation culminates with a superb speech by Robert Haas, Chairman of the Board and CEO of Levi Strauss & Company. As we go through it together, you will see what goes into a first-class speech, and how skillfully points can be made and then woven together. By gaining this understanding, you will enjoy the benefit of Haas's example for many, many presentations to come.

Because *The Perfect Presentation* takes you through a process, you will get the most from it if you follow the process from beginning to end, at least the first time. Try not to skip, even parts that might seem irrelevant at the time. Trust that everything has been included for a purpose and that this purpose will emerge.

After the first reading, feel free to concentrate on the parts you need the most. The flowcharts will remind you of the context.

Naturally, you will want to work through your weaknesses. But don't neglect your strengths. Your strengths are what give you confidence, and your best qualities are what will make you outstanding.

The Perfect Presentation contains many fill-in exercises. They're extremely important, so answer them in writing. You may want to use pencil, in order to erase and use them again. It might be an even better idea to make photocopies of the exercises for future use.

IN THE BEGINNING

ALL GREAT SPEAKERS WERE BAD SPEAKERS AT FIRST.

—*Ralph Waldo Emerson*

A presentation can be anything from a two-second announcement ("The king is dead! Long live the king!") to the closing ceremonies of the Olympic Games. Most of the time you will be aiming for something in between.

Because a presentation is such a highly complex human interaction, it has the same potential for excitement and disaster as a moon launch, a dinner party, or a seduction. When you make a presentation, you are the scientist, host, and lover combined, with more than a bit of the showman thrown in.

Perhaps you have a terrific message, but you're not sure how to deliver it. Or maybe your immediate need is to say something—anything—to a waiting audience, and you can't imagine how to get started.

The Perfect Presentation assumes that you are about to create and deliver your presentation all by yourself. Maybe you're not. Possibly you will be a "power behind the throne," putting together script packages for others to deliver. Or you may be delivering a performance scripted by someone else. In any case, your results will be enhanced by understanding what goes into the solo process.

The Growing Importance of Presentations

We are entering the age of what Peter Drucker calls "the information-based organization." The way people work together is changing dramatically. More and more projects are being done in *synchrony*, by "task-focused" teams consisting of small groups of specialists from different fields, who collaborate on projects from beginning to end.

Because members of these *ad hoc* teams do not share common frames of reference, communication skills become critical. No way can R&D people, computer programmers, manufacturers and marketers catch up on their progress over a long lunch, or make do with memos. What they need are frequent, systematic, and thorough explanations from one another, with plenty of charts and graphs and pictures, along with the chance to ask questions. In other words, they need presentations.

It doesn't stop there either. Presentations may be needed again when reports are made to headquarters or the team is invited to present its results at national or international conferences. In an information-based world, you can't advance if you can't present. There's simply no safe place to hide.

You Can Get There from Here

Maybe you are relatively at ease in front of others, yet aware that somehow your presentations fall flat. Or maybe you suffer agonies of sweaty palms and churning intestines at the very thought of getting up to speak. Possibly you're fine with small groups but paralyzed in front of a crowd— or inspired in front of a crowd but tongue-tied with one or two. You could be a fledgling manager dreading your first report to a committee, or an experienced executive who turns to jelly at the sight of a video camera.

Whatever, you're in good company. Anxiety about speaking in public is the single most common fear, far surpassing the dread of disease, death, or nuclear war. This anxiety takes many forms and comes in many intensities, but it usually has two common causes: *no training or poor training, and fears that seem more rational than they are.*

Bustles and Stovepipe Hats

When school budgets are cut, "public speaking" is one of the first "frills" to go. Where it is still taught, it may be taught in ways that do more harm than good. You may have been trained to use an artificial tone, hold your hands still, look past your audience, speak from rote memory, or read from a text—in other words, to give presentations in the style of a century ago. Using that style today is as ludicrous and uncomfortable as wearing a bustle or a stovepipe hat. Yet it may be the only style you know.

An Audience of Monsters

You may dread facing an audience as if it consisted of ogres from a childhood dream. Perhaps you rationalize this fear on the grounds that your whole future hangs on how you will give your presentation. Yet, if you looked back, you would probably remember plenty of other occasions when you experienced the same dread, even though very little was at stake. Besides, as you know perfectly well, most careers are determined by many, many factors, and not by any one particular speech.

Taking Action on Two Fronts

Fighting a two-front war on one front only is a losing strategy. Making presentations also requires aggressive action on two fronts. The emotional factors need to be worked on, right along with the mastery of a modern presentation style. My experience in training speakers has shown that this psychological-plus-practical approach can be powerful. In remarkably little time, people begin to express themselves comfortably and effectively—and even enjoy themselves doing it.

If it could happen to Michael, it can happen to you.

Michael—a VP Revisits Kindergarten

A programming prodigy with a brand-new computer science M.A. from Stanford, Michael had been invited to join a fledgling Silicon Valley company. Four years later, the company had grown from a dozen people working intimately together into a burgeoning enterprise with nearly two hundred employees and a corporate chain of command. Michael was now in charge of a department of some forty people, several of them with doctorates.

At first Michael thrived on his new responsibilities. He had no trouble managing his first few assistants, or the next few after that. Whenever necessary, he'd poke his nose in. "Joe, you're doing a great job. Keep on doing what you're doing." "Eddie, I think it might go better if you tried it this way." Informality was his style.

But when it became a matter of twenty people, then thirty, then forty, it became impossible to manage them so casually. Only so much could be done through private meetings and departmental memos. Michael knew he had to start assembling his people for meetings. In fact, the change was long overdue.

The problem was, *he couldn't.* Like many researchers and innovators, Michael was a private, introverted person. The thought of getting up before forty seated and expectant people, even his own subordinates, literally made him sick. He got even sicker when he thought of the rapidly expanding board of directors, not to mention the invitation to speak before a convention back East.

Michael knew he had a problem and decided to do something about it. He called the Human Resources and Training Department. "Do you have a seminar that would help me talk in public?"

It so happened that I was about to give a seminar for the company's managers. Michael was the first to sign up.

The depth of his difficulty became obvious on the second day. The trainees had been assigned to prepare a short speech. When Michael's turn came, he literally could not get out a word. The best he could manage was a pathetic grunt that sounded like *uh-uh-uh*.

I called Michael down from the podium and sat him in a chair facing me. He tried to say something, but still could not get out a coherent sound. Instinct and experience told me that anything that went so deep had to be very ancient. I decided to aim right at the target area.

JM: Just make yourself comfortable, Michael. Ignore those other people. They're not there.

M: . . .

JM: Okay. Now, when you were little, I bet you were up on a stage once, right?

M: *(reluctantly nods)*

JM: I bet it was in first grade. Or maybe in kindergarten.

M: *(looks as if I had struck him)*

JM: In kindergarten, was it? I bet it was a play. Was it a play? A special play. A Christmas play?

M: *(nodding)* Uh-uh.

JM: And all the other kids were watching. And the other kids' parents. And your own parents too. Right?

M: *(nodding)* Uh-uh-uh.

JM: And you were standing there in front of them. And you couldn't remember your lines. You thought you'd die, right? All you wanted was to get off that stage any way you could.

M: *(practically in tears)* Uh-uh-uh.

JM: So you did what any five-year-old would do, to get off the stage. You just stood there and cried till somebody led you off. Right?

M: *(nodding with relief)* Uh-uh.

(Now we knew the source of his panic. Time to direct him to a more adult and effective way of handling it.)

JM: Okay, Michael. That was a long time ago. You have other choices now besides standing there and crying, don't you?

M: ? ? ?

JM: For example, you could write out everything you want to say and have someone else read it for you. That would work, right? Or you can have the head of each project get up and make a report and answer all the questions. That would help, wouldn't it?

M: *(forgetting he "can't" talk)* Yeah. Right.

JM: Or you can . . . Let's see, can you help me out? I'm drawing a blank. What else could you do if you didn't feel up to making a formal speech about something?

M: I guess I could tell them I'd lost my speech but I'd be glad to answer any questions.

JM: And that would be okay with you?

M: Sure. No problem.

JM: You could get up and on that stage right now and just answer questions about your topic? So long as you didn't have to read anything off or say it from memory?

M: Sure. No problem.

JM: Okay. Go ahead and do it.

And so he did. Michael got up before the group, announced his topic, and asked for questions. By handling them well, he discovered that he had broken his "taboo" about being on stage. He didn't have to "lecture" anyone, and what a relief that was. All he had to do was answer questions. With his remarkable memory, that was no problem. And since he was a pleasant, unassuming person, people were sure to speak up and remind him in case he forgot something.

Michael was now over the single biggest hurdle. He no longer dreaded the thought of speaking to a group, at least in a casual, informal way. Of course, he still had to master the techniques and attitudes that would allow him to give more formal presentations.

Highly encouraged, Michael put in his homework, practice, and time. In the end, he blossomed into a confident and enthusiastic presenter.

Fallback Strategies

When it came to almost anything but giving presentations, Michael was an effective, successful person. He was certainly not neurotic or disturbed. His seemingly bizarre behavior in the seminar was merely an exaggeration of the panic that most of the trainees were feeling.

Finding ways around the act of presentation was not a special strategy devised just for Michael. It was for everyone. Under any panic circumstance, having a fallback position is one of the best means there is for reducing pressure and regaining control.

People overcoming freeway phobias first begin by driving in the right lane. It calms them to know they can pull off onto the shoulder for a minute or even take the next exit if the tension becomes too much. They may never actually do it, but knowing that they *can* soothes anxiety and allows them to keep on driving. In planning any kind of difficult or risky enterprise, it is often wise to plan fallback positions and strategic retreats. As the old saying goes, "He who fights and runs away lives to fight another day."

The Enigma of Anxiety and Boredom

Presentations *ought* to be exciting. They tell us what has been happening in our workplace, events that affect our livelihood and thus our very survival. They tell us what is happening here, now, and in the universe beyond. What could possibly be more compelling?

And yet, for many of us, presentations are associated with the worst sort of anxiety and boredom—anxiety for the speaker and boredom for those who must listen. Why should this be?

We have all encountered riveting speakers who make us hang on every word. These people are not necessarily good-looking, or gifted with great voices, or even particularly brilliant. What they do have is a clear sense of purpose, a purpose that communicates directly with our minds and hearts. Such people teach us what presentations can be like and should be like—and would be like, if only more speakers knew what they were doing.

What Goes Wrong and What Goes Right

Speakers get anxious because they are unprepared. Either they don't believe in their material or they don't believe in themselves. And listeners get bored because unprepared speakers are boring.

To go out there and give a presentation worth hearing, you have to be dead certain about two things:

1. What you want to achieve
2. Your own fitness to achieve it

Before you step out in front of your audience, your purpose, and its worthiness, must be blazingly clear in your mind. Your conviction, fervent or discreet, will then become the catalyst for firing your audience with an equal enthusiasm.

The subject of your next presentation must have seemed important to someone, or it would never have been scheduled. As the presenter, it is your job to keep that sense of importance alive, and to pass it on, like an Olympic torch.

What Is a Presentation?

A presentation is a spoken communication made in a prepared and formal way. Among the almost countless kinds of presentations you may be called upon to make are these:

Making a progress report to your supervisor

    Or your support staff

    Or your board of directors

Explaining a product or service to a new client

    Or an established client

    Or a company that might license it

Lecturing trainees

    Or your whole department

    Or an international conference

Presenting yourself for a job interview

    Or an audition

    Or the review of a project

These represent very different circumstances, calling for different degrees of preparation and formality. What is the common factor? What makes them all *presentations?* The answer is at once simple and a bit disconcerting:

A presentation requires a much higher level of performance than casual conversation. It also provides for advance time to achieve that higher level.

A Presentation Is an Unnatural Act

If human beings were as rational as *Star Trek*'s Mr. Spock, this would constitute no problem. The more advance time given, the better the performance would be. But human beings are Earthlings, not Vulcans. Human anxieties feed on the awareness that a high level of performance is expected. And the longer the advance time, the fatter the anxieties may grow.

It is in the nature of speech to be spontaneous and unrehearsed. Having to plan a normally spontaneous act can lead to self-consciousness and performance anxiety. Ask any lover.

Worse yet, a speaker knows that the spotlight will be on him and him alone. It's the stuff of nightmares.

To make matters yet worse, important things hang in the balance. The speaker is distracted from his subject by worries about his appearance, reputation, self-esteem, and even the future direction of his career.

And yet there are people who thrive under these pressures. How do they do it?

THE FOUR STAGES OF PREPARATION

Confident speakers look upon presentations as opportunities—chances to organize their thinking and share their ideas. Consciously or not, all of them go through the same *Four Stages of the Track-and-Field Model:*

They prepare themselves in head and heart. (GET READY)

They assess their particular audience. (ON YOUR MARK)

They organize what they are going to do. (GET SET)

They begin and end in a memorable way. (GO)

Confident presenters will move through these stages so gracefully that the results seem spontaneous. When called upon to speak extemporaneously, they can go through the whole process in a manner of seconds. They are able to get right to their feet and speak effortlessly and well. They show enjoyment in what they are doing, and the pleasure is contagious. In an imperfect world, you can't come closer to perfection than that.

Follow their methods, and you will soon be giving perfect presentations too.

Chapter One

GET READY

THE READINESS IS ALL.

—Shakespeare

RIPENESS IS ALL.

—Shakespeare

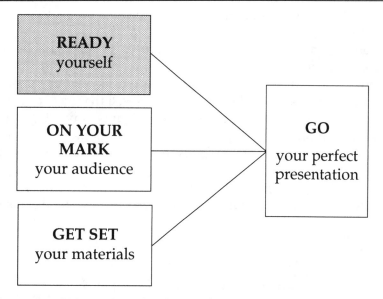

Shakespeare believed in the force of readiness so profoundly that he wrote of it twice. Ever since, successful generals, entrepreneurs, and therapists have been confirming his conviction. Only when someone is truly ready for something will it happen—whether it be surging to victory, closing that deal, or falling in love. The tricky part is getting to the ready state.

When it comes to presentations, there are two aspects to readiness. Your head must be ready, and so must your heart.

Head-Readiness

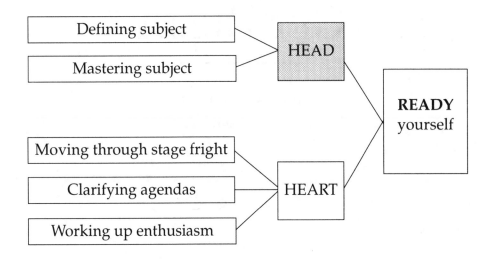

From Purpose to Mastery

Head-readiness means having a clear purpose. It also means doing your homework and knowing your stuff.

In theory, this is a simple and logical procedure. If your purpose is to sell a product, you learn to demonstrate it so well that its use seems easy and attractive. You memorize the facts and figures, advantages and disadvantages, not only of that product but its competitors. You master a script. You prepare answers to likely questions. You rehearse proven closes.

Public speaking and presentations before groups are somewhat more complicated. Neither your purpose nor what you have to learn is so cut-and-dried.

Defining Your Subject

When asked what single event was most helpful in developing the theory of relativity, Albert Einstein . . . answered, "Figuring out how to think about the problem."

—*Wilbur Schramm and William Porter,*
Men, Women, Messages and Media

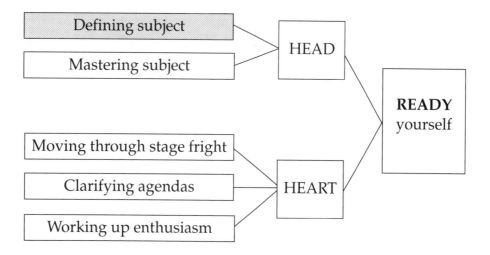

Sometimes your subject is clearly defined from the start. Sometimes it isn't, and you only discover it as you go along. At still other times, you'll begin with one clear intention and later shift to another.

For example, you are to report to a committee on research in progress. Your subject seems (and may be) obvious: you will describe and explain the results you have achieved so far. But what if you discover anomalies in your data? You may have to change direction and report on *them*. Or what if you suddenly come up with the solution for a problem? That solution might now become the subject of your report.

Ways and Means

You have to start somewhere. You have to begin with a subject even though you know it may change. The more exactly you have defined it, the more readily it can be confirmed or altered later on.

Start by deciding what you hope to achieve. Define the practical intention your presentation will serve. Ask yourself two questions, and answer them in writing.

The Initial Intention Miniquiz

What do my listeners not know that I wish to tell them? _____

_____

_____

_____

What particular issues or aspects do I need to emphasize? _____

_____

_____

_____

_____

Keep going back to these questions for as long as you are working on your presentation. And don't be too shocked if you start coming up with different answers.

The Five Patterns of Organization

Your answers to these questions will determine the ultimate form, or structure, of your presentation. In architecture, the watchword is: *Form follows function.* It helps to think of a speech in the same way: *Structure follows purpose.*

There are five basic types of structure, *five patterns of organization,* each performing a specific function:

The Five Patterns and Their Uses

1. *Problem*—moves to action and solution
2. *Opinion*—persuades
3. *Thesis*—proves
4. *Instruction*—tells how
5. *Information*—provides facts

Consider your purpose and decide which pattern describes it best. Expect that there will be hybrids. You are going to have to provide facts in order to persuade or prove or suggest solutions to a problem. You are going to have to persuade listeners that a problem exists. But first comes the decision as to which is your primary goal.

What is your *main* goal? To get people to join you in solving a *problem?* To state your *opinion* regarding some controversy? To present factual evidence to prove a *thesis?* To give *instruction* on how to do something? To provide updated *information?*

Define and redefine your purpose until you know which describes it best. Know the reasons you have chosen the particular pattern of organization you have.

Pattern Summary

I am presenting my subject as _____ a problem, _____ an opinion, _____ a thesis, _____ instruction, _____ information, because: _____

_____

_____

_____

_____

By the time you're ready to put together your presentation, you may have decided on another approach. But for now at least, you have a direction.

MASTERING YOUR SUBJECT

RAW DATA CAN BE, BUT ISN'T NECESSARILY INFORMA-
TION. . . . INFORMATION MUST BE THAT WHICH LEADS
TO UNDERSTANDING. IF IT DOESN'T MAKE SENSE TO
YOU, IT DOESN'T QUALIFY.

—*Richard Saul Wurman*, Information Anxiety

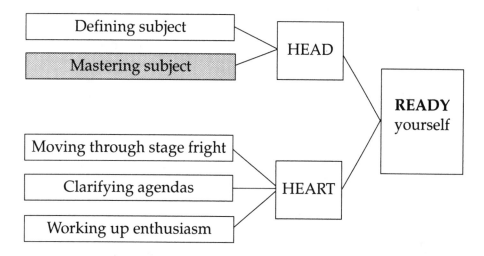

Head-readiness begins with the subject and ends with mastery. *The subject* asks the questions. *Mastery* provides the answers.

You achieve mastery by doing your homework and assimilating the results. Unfortunately, this may be harder for you than it should be.

Millions of people, including many with advanced degrees, have never learned how to learn. They are like people without keys trying to force their way through doors, and wasting precious time and energy in the process.

If this is your problem, you are not alone. Poor learning habits are a national epidemic.

Three Steps to Mastery

To learn a subject, any subject, these three simple steps will give the best return for your time:

1. **Focus your attention.**
2. **Remember through comprehension.**
3. **Test and question yourself.**

Focus Your Attention

When you plan a serious meeting, you write the time in your calendar and ask the switchboard to hold your calls. You do this because the human mind, like the human eye, focuses best on one thing at a time. Your presentation deserves the same priority.

Try thinking of your attention as money in the bank. The more you spend on one thing, the less you have left to spend on another.

Remember Through Comprehension

There are two ways to learn, through rote and through comprehension.

Rote learning hammers sequences of noises into the memory. (Columbus discovered America in . . . *1492*. Two times two equals . . . *four*.)

Comprehension provides a context for, an understanding of, what is memorized.

Rote learning has its uses, but only in a context of comprehension. If you haven't the foggiest notion where Columbus came from, why he made the trip, or what "America" was like when he "discovered" it, the date *1492* won't tell you much. And a non-English speaker—or a parrot for that matter—can be taught "two-times-two-equals-four" in English and be none the wiser for it.

The great question with all learning is *So what?* If you can't answer that, you are nowhere. Closed-minded persons ask *So what?* insolently, implying that there is no answer. Asked politely but persistently, *So what?* is a magic question. It assumes there is an answer and you intend to find it.

Comprehension organizes details. The better you understand the larger picture, the more easily small facts will fall into place. It's like putting together a jigsaw. Once you can imagine the complete puzzle, you know where to fit the pieces.

Test and Question Yourself

You can't ask *So what?* often enough. Begin at the beginning. *Why did the writer of this report give it the name she did?* First paragraphs are particularly rich. *Why start here? What's the purpose? What's she trying to establish?*

Deal with your material aggressively. Hang in there until you feel you understand. When you don't, formulate questions and write them down. Ask the printed word, ask other people, ask your own mind for answers—then write them down too. Human beings think pretty much alike. By formulating and asking questions, you not only clarify your own mind, you also arm yourself for any challenges the audience may throw at you.

By the way, if you can't find any satisfactory answer, congratulations. You have discovered a whole new subject.

HEART-READINESS

THE ASPIRATION AND DETERMINATION OF AN ATHLETE TO SUCCEED WHEN HIS BODY IS RUINED, OF AN ENGINEER TO BUILD AGAIN WHEN HIS BRIDGE FALLS DOWN, OF A NATION TO PROSPER AFTER ITS ECONOMY HAS CRASHED, OR OF A SCIENTIST TO CONDUCT YEARS OF UNSUCCESSFUL EXPERIMENTS HELP US UNDERSTAND THE ORIGINS OF SUCCESS.

—*Richard Saul Wurman,* Information Anxiety

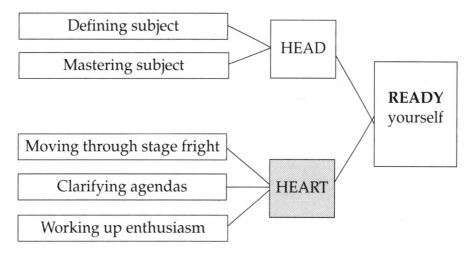

Attitude is everything. The best-prepared head will get you nowhere without a ready heart.

Heart-readiness comes from the courage, confidence, and enthusiasm that bring presentations to life. Emotion is highly contagious. If you are nervous, bored, or dying-to-get-the-whole-thing-done-with, your listeners will feel the same. But if you are stimulated, chances are they will be too.

The process of heart-readiness begins with clearing away barriers—distracting personal agendas and that complex of inhibitions known as stage fright.

Moving Through Stage Fright

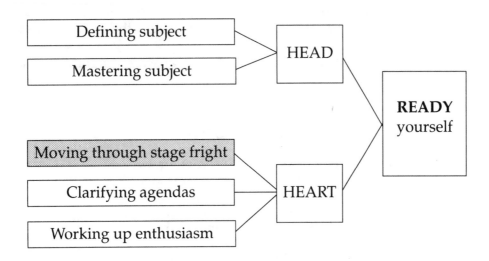

Stage Fright and the Olivier Moment

If you are nervous about facing an audience, you have plenty of company. Even a great actor, the late Sir Laurence Olivier, confessed to moments of nauseating panic. Yet, once he stepped on the stage he forgot his anxiety and lost himself in his role.

Olivier could do this because he was head-ready. He knew his lines cold. He was thoroughly rehearsed. He could be sure that once he got started, his preparation would take over and carry him. He would be able to ride it all the way to the final curtain.

The Power of the Presenter

In an age of information, knowledge is power. But power without this means to convey it is worthless.

Perfect presenters are many things. Like great actors or comedians, they stir others to passion and laughter. Like great teachers, they pass on knowledge and information. Like great statesmen and religious leaders, they change the ways we think and act.

Nerves? Or Just Excitement?

One of the strangest things about our emotions is that we don't always know what they are. When adrenaline gets loose in our system, we shake, our knees turn to water, our hearts pound, we get dizzy, we sweat. Familiar symptoms, but of what?

These same symptoms strike whether we're about to embrace our beloved, have been condemned to the gallows, have just escaped an auto accident or won the lottery. It's usually the context that tells us whether we're in agony or ecstasy.

Perhaps what you think of as fear is at least partly excitement. Or the other way round. It's all what you tell yourself, after all. Your body doesn't know the difference.

Stage Fright and the Fear of Inadequacy

Possibly you feel your ideas or knowledge are inadequate. Or that you lack charisma or authority. Maybe you're even afraid people will laugh.

Perhaps you were raised by people who put you down: *"Look who's talking!" "Who do you think you are?"*

Expectations

Most of us tend to perform as we expect to perform. But where do our expectations come from?

Ultimately, they come from others. As small children, we learn what we are taught. If we are taught to think well of ourselves, we usually do. Likewise, we absorb the lessons that undermine us. Most of us manage to pick up some of both, believing in ourselves and doubting ourselves at the same time.

Self-doubt torments even the most highly accomplished people. Take the case of Moira, who worked for the Equal Rights Commission.

Moira—a Ghost Story

Moira was scheduled to speak to the department heads of a large corporation, and she was terrified. She could not make sense of her dread, as she had often addressed corporate bodies before.

In the privacy of my office, Moira was able to discuss her upcoming speech with ease and conviction. Her message was simple: the company, which relied in part on federal funds, would have to start hiring more women or be in violation of the law. Yet, somehow, she was afraid to say this. Moira, a brilliant, capable woman, felt she could not face doing this very simple thing.

My first task was to coax her into a recognition of her problem. This was done with simple questions.

JM: Is what you have to say important?
M: It sure is.
JM: Is it something you think they'll be glad to hear?
M: Oh, no. They want to hire whom they want to hire, and that's mainly men.
JM: Then why should they listen?
M: Because if they don't, they'll be breaking the law. There may be fines and penalties.
JM: So it's to their benefit to hear it, even though they may not want to?
M: That's right.
JM: But you're uncomfortable delivering this unpopular message?
M: Uh-huh.
JM: Are you always this uncomfortable delivering unpopular messages?
M: No. Actually not.
JM: Then it's this particular message? To this particular audience?
M: Yes. It seems to be.
    (Now it was time to probe into the causes.)
JM: Moira, look out the window at those trees. Imagine they're the department heads. Who are they? Are they men or women?
M: Mostly men. Almost all men.
JM: Is there any one of them you have particular trouble talking to?
M: Yes. That one. He's like my father.
JM: What would your father say, Moira, if he heard you deliver that message?
M: He'd say, "Moira, look at you. You're twenty-eight years old. You're throwing your life away on this women's lib stuff. You have no husband, no children. If you don't hurry up, you'll never have them. You'll end up a lonely old maid.
JM: How do you feel about that, Moira? Do you agree with your father?
M: (after some thought) No. I believe in women's rights.
JM: If you don't get married before you're thirty, are you going to feel like a failure?
M: Maybe. A little.
JM: Will you separate your feelings about that from the task of speaking to the chairmen?
M: (with relief) Yes.
    (Now she was ready to move ahead into taking action.)
JM: Will you imagine telling your father he doesn't belong here?
M: Sure. Why not?

JM: Will you imagine going down to where he is and politely escorting him to the door?

M: All right.

JM: *(after some seconds)* Is he still in the audience, Moira?

M: No.

JM: Give your speech now, for the others.

M: Okay. I'd like to.

(By this time, Moira was quite excited by the prospect. She rehearsed her speech with conviction and confidence. Now all she needed was some reinforcement.)

JM: You were fine. Now, when you're in front of your audience, if you see your "father" there, will you show him to the door again?

M: Sure. Why not!

JM: Remember, in reality it would take a few minutes. But we're dealing with fantasy here. It can take as little time as necessary. Even a fraction of a second if that's all you have.

M: Yes. I understand.

When the scheduled day arrived, Moira went ahead and delivered her talk to the department heads without difficulty.

Family Conditioning

Habits of fear and failure can be instituted at an early age. An interactive, verbal family that has lively discussions will produce assertive adults who feel entitled to their opinions and easy about expressing them.

When President Kennedy was a child, his parents were something of a laughing stock among their friends for the raucous scenes at the family table. During dinner, toddlers hardly out of diapers vied with their brothers, sisters, and parents in asserting opinions on anything from sports to books to politics. Family friends might have scoffed, but the Kennedy children grew up to be fearless public speakers, expressing themselves as naturally as they breathed.

In contrast disapproving parents, like Moira's father, promote blocks in their children. Fortunately, as the experience of hundreds of my own trainees has proved, these blocks can be overcome.

Dear Old Golden Rule Days

Tactless teachers can be as destructive as tactless parents, especially since their put-downs take place in public. A very small dose of classroom trauma can go a long way.

Two weeks into second grade, seven-year-old David suddenly lost his usually self-contained manner and began complaining of stomach pains in the morning. Patient questioning by his mother brought out the cause.

D: Mommy, please. I don't want to talk about it.
M: Why not?
D: You'll get mad.
M: Do I usually get mad at you when you're unhappy about something?
D: No. But I just can't.
M: Why not?
D: It will hurt your feelings.
M: Don't worry about my feelings. Let's talk about yours.
D: *(after prolonged agony)* I went to school dirty.
M: *(truly bewildered)* You what?
D: I mean, I left the house clean, but I played on the way and got dirty.
M: And you didn't wash up?
D: Right. I'm sorry.
M: You know, that's not so terrible.
D: *(fighting tears)* But when I raised my hand to ask a question, Miss Pettis pulled me to the front of the whole class and showed them.
M: What did she say?
D: She said I was a disgrace coming to school dirty. She said, didn't my mother know better than to let me come to school that way? *(bursting into tears)* I tried telling her it wasn't your fault, but she wouldn't listen.
M: And is that all? Or has there been more?
D: Yes. I worry so much she'll do it again that I can't concentrate. Then she yells at me for not paying attention. In front of everybody.
M: And that's why you've been getting sick in the mornings? Because you're afraid she'll treat you like that again?
D: I guess so.
M: David, you should have washed up, but this is all out of proportion. You stay home today. I'll go in and talk to Miss Pettis—and to your principal too.

Over David's embarrassed protests, his mother saw Miss Pettis that noon. The teacher declared that David was immature, seemed emotionally disturbed and possibly retarded. The mother was astounded. David had always been exceptionally precocious. He was an avid, fluent reader and had scored over 160 on an IQ test at the private school which he had attended to this time.

David's mother told all this to Miss Pettis, who was not impressed. David's mother, she said, was "deluded by love." David's mother went to the principal and insisted that her son be transferred to another teacher. Within days of his transfer, David went to the top of his class and stayed there.

Twenty years later, David holds a Ph.D. from Harvard and gives presentations of his scientific research before international audiences. But what if his mother had failed to respond so promptly when he was seven? What if he had spent an entire year being treated like a disturbed, retarded child? What if he had gone on into third grade with that reputation and self-image?

Millions of other children have been less lucky than David, and handicapped through insensitive treatment. How many remember back to the root cause, or connect it with their dread of making themselves conspicuous?

You may be one of them. Seemingly trivial events from your earliest days may still be shackling you, as they shackled Michael and Moira. You may think your problem is something inborn, while it is merely ingrained.

Playing Detective with Blocks from Childhood

The procedures I used with Moira and Michael—and which David's mother used with her son—are really quite simple and can be learned and self-applied. They consist of a series of gently probing questions, each one shaped to a large extent by the preceding answer.

Next time you are anxious about a specific presentation, or just anxious about presentations in general, put yourself through the following exercise.

Exorcism #1—The Demons of Stage Fright

Why are you giving this presentation?

_____

_____

_____

_____

Why will the listeners be listening?

_____

_____

_____

_____

Is it to their benefit to listen?

_____

_____

If it's to their benefit to listen, why are you reluctant to share?

_____

_____

_____

_____

Are you always this uncomfortable, or is it worse this time?

_____

Imagine the audience is now in front of you. Who are they?

_____

Are they mainly men or women?

_____

Does that make a difference?

_____

Why?

_____

_____

Look at your audience again. Is there any one of them you would have particular trouble talking to?

_____

Who is it?

_____

What would that person say if that person heard your presentation?

_____

_____

_____

_____

_____

_____

How do you feel about that? Do you agree?

_____

_____

_____

How long have you known this person?

_____

Does he remind you of anyone else you've known longer?

_____

Who?

_____

How old were you when you remember first feeling like this?

_____

What happened?

_____

_____

_____

_____

_____

_____

_____

Will you separate your feelings about what that person said or what you felt then from your goals in making your presentation?

_____

Will you imagine yourself telling that person that he or she doesn't belong in your audience?

_____

Go down to where that person is, and politely escort that person out.

_____

Go back to the stage and notice that the person is no longer in the audience. Now give your speech for the rest.

Notes on Exorcisms

If you saw the movie *The Exorcist*, you must know that demons are seldom driven out with a single try. The process takes persistence and repetition. You may have to repeat the preceding exercise any number of times, perhaps coming up with the same unwelcome listener, perhaps various ones. After all, few of us have been lucky enough to experience childhoods marred by only one destructive moment or discouraging person.

Each time you go through the exercise, you will achieve greater clarity. You will see that the harsh self-image you may be carrying is not a God's-eye judgment but merely a child's interpretation of the thoughtless words of some all-too-human parent or teacher.

Avoidance as Self-Protection

Avoiding public presentations is a way of not being judged. So long as that nagging, critical inner voice keeps telling you, "Nothing you do will be good enough. *You're* not good enough," you will avoid making the effort to grow and change. The adult in you will continue to be controlled by the child. The present and the future will remain hostage to the past.

Just Whom Are You Trying to Impress?

As we have seen from Moira's example, the audience actually in front of you is not necessarily the one you will be speaking to in your head. More likely than not, you will be trying to impress, please, or placate someone else.

It may be a parent. Or a teacher. Or your clergyman. Or some imagined circle of experts. Or your lover, spouse, or ex-spouse. Or your friends. Or even, as we will consider shortly, your high school class.

Authorities from Childhood

Parents, grade-school teachers, and clergy are authority figures, carried within us from long ago. If we are speaking so as to please (or not offend) these authorities, then it is the fearful child in us that will be getting up to make the presentation. Those ghosts from the past, if not too over-whelmingly persistent, are best dealt with by exorcism exercises, such as the one I have already introduced. In cases where they outlast your most persistent attempts to get rid of them, personal counseling may be useful.

"Supreme Courts"

Other imaginary audiences develop somewhat later in life, in our teens or even adulthood. These are circles of experts, fearsomely wise and all-knowing beings whom we appoint to be the final judges of our work and worth. A surprising number of highly able people strive hopelessly to win before such "Supreme Courts," looking upon them as the only audience worth courting.

Derek—a Horror Story

Derek, an immensely successful horror novelist, once lectured a creative writing seminar in San Antonio. The greater part of his speech was a lamentation over the refusal of prestigious critics, such as writers for the *New York Review of Books* and the *New York Times Book Review,* to take his novels seriously, along with the failure of English professors at Ivy League colleges to assign them. Why didn't they realize that his supernatural characters were *symbols?* Why couldn't they understand that he was writing *literature?*

A fan spoke up from the audience. "What do you care about a bunch of newspaper reviewers and college teachers? Don't you know that any one of them would give an arm and a leg to have written just one of your books? Don't you know your work is wonderful? That we read it because we love it, not because it's been assigned?"

But the famous writer did not know his work was "wonderful." As a college freshman, perhaps, listening to some fervent instructor swear by the *Times* and heap scorn on popular "trash," he had decided that "wonderful" books were those prized by dazzling minds like the instructor's. Or perhaps, at that age, already determined to be a writer, he had started reading the *New York Review of Books,* yearning to become the object of its fulsome flatteries, dreading to be the target of its scathing contempt.

His favorite teachers and the critics he admired became the audience he wrote for. Winning their praise, being accepted into their circle, became his definition of success. Not having achieved that, he felt like a failure, no matter how many copies he sold, or how many millions he made, or how enthusiastic his readership might be.

Loved Ones

People we love come in two sizes, those big enough to want to see us grow and flourish, and those small enough to be threatened by our success.

For the most part, our big-sized loved ones are a blessing. They assist us. They encourage us. They take pride in us. They rejoice with us in our accomplishments. Their enthusiastic support enhances our victories because it allows them to be shared.

Sometimes, however, big-sized loved ones can get a bit *too* big. They can try to live through us, or overwhelm us with obligations. Or they can expect more than we are able to deliver, and leave us feeling that nothing we do will ever be good enough.

Small-sized loved ones are an unmitigated disaster. Whether they are parents or siblings or lovers or spouses, they can't bear the thought of our outshining or outgrowing them. If we attempt anything outside our range, they throw words at us like "arrogant" or "snob" or "stuck-up" or "smart-ass" or "disloyal," or even worse. They demand confessions that *we think we are better than they are.* They pick quarrels or abandon us and refuse to speak. They may even sabotage our careers.

Richard—Heartbreak Hotel

Richard was a corporate vice president about to leave for Europe to meet with the company's European division and speak to a convention on a major project. This trip represented a great step forward in his career and he was both excited and uneasy. His wife, an aspiring artist with not much success to show for her efforts, chose the eve of his departure to announce that she was in love with another man. Richard was so devastated that he was a distracted wreck throughout the trip; he paced his hotel rooms all night, stumbled through his presentation, and generally made a poor impression.

When he returned in despair, his wife told him that she had given up her lover and wanted only to save the marriage. She also claimed that the timing of her announcement, although unfortunate, had been purely coincidental. Richard did not know what to think. With his career in shambles, he threw himself into "saving" his marriage. It took several months of marriage counseling before he realized that he must leave his envious and destructive partner.

After that, he began recovering lost ground. A two-day seminar helped him to get past his trauma-induced unease with making presentations. Wanting a fresh start, he moved to another company where he is once again flourishing.

Adrienne—a Bad Bargain

Sometimes even ex-spouses can undo us. Adrienne, a professional speaker, came to me because she had begun to choke up and lose her voice when speaking before a group. She found herself constantly clearing her throat, even though she knew that nothing irritated the vocal cords more. It occurred to me that something was "stuck" in her throat, perhaps something she wanted badly to say. I set about finding out what it was, through a process of elimination:

JM: How are things at home, Adrienne?
A: They're okay.
JM: How's Jack?
A: Wonderful. He's a joy.
JM: How long have you two been together now?
A: Two years next month. It's still like a honeymoon.
JM: How are your kids? Both in college now, aren't they?
A: Right. They're doing great.

JM: And what about your first husband? Is that over?

A: Well, no. Not exactly.

JM: Something you want to tell him?

A: Sort of. In a way. Mark keeps phoning me. He wants to talk about himself. What he's doing.

JM: That's not all right with you?

A: No. It's not at all.

JM: Why not?

A: I get the distinct feeling he's still hoping we'll get back together. And that's never going to happen.

JM: Adrienne, imagine he's sitting in that empty chair and tell him out loud what you want to change.

A: "Look, Mark. We're finished with our marriage. We'll always be connected through the children, but I can't be a part of your ongoing life. I don't want to keep hearing about every detail."

JM: What would happen if you actually said that?

A: . . .

JM: (after a pause) What do you feel while you listen to him?

A: Rage.

JM: Hang up.

A: I can't.

JM: Why not?

A: Because he might stop paying the kids' tuition.

JM: Pretty high price you're paying for that tuition, wouldn't you say? Do you think it's an appropriate price?

A: . . .

JM: Is it worth all this anxiety, Adrienne? Worth closing up your throat?

A: Crazy, isn't it? I'm still afraid of depriving my kids.

JM: This is the only way your kids can go to college, is that it? He pays, or they don't go to school?

A: (laughing in spite of herself) Actually they're pretty motivated, both of them. Resourceful too. I suppose they'd manage to get through somehow, no matter what.

JM: Even if he stopped paying, and you couldn't afford to, they'd still manage?

A: Yes. They'd manage.

JM: So, are you willing to close off the relationship with your ex-husband, even at the risk that he will stop paying their tuition?

A: Yes. You know, I had no idea that's why I was losing my voice.

JM: Adrienne, do you know any good voice-loosening exercises?

A: Sure. Use them all the time.

JM: Could you show me a couple now?

A: (smiling) Be glad to.

She proceeded to blow air through her lips in a prolonged Bronx cheer, followed by blowing baby bubbles. Her voice came through clearly and well, though broken up by a good deal of laughter. Then I asked her to give me some of her upcoming presentation, which she did fluently.

High School Confidential

Adolescents are the greatest conformists in the world. They may rebel against their parents, or defy God and the law, but they find it virtually impossible to stand up against their peers. To be considered a jerk or a nerd, to be weird or unpopular, is about the worst fate that can befall a person of fifteen.

Unfortunately, high school culture in this country is profoundly anti-intellectual and anti-accomplishment. Except when it comes to sports, beauty, or spending money, it is frequently disastrous to stand above the crowd. Students who show enthusiasm for their work are labeled with ugly names. They may even feel ashamed of being competent. Girls with top grades fear they won't be asked for dates. Boys with top grades feel put down in comparison with football heroes.

Movies and television have been reinforcing these destructive values for generations. From *Cynthia* back in the forties, to *Dirty Dancing* in the eighties, the girl at the top of her class, however gorgeous, must throw aside her books and social position and get out there and boogie, if she wants to catch a real hunk. Likewise, in movies from *East of Eden* to *Grease* and beyond, it's the sullen hunk of a dropout who takes the desirable girl away from the pompous valedictorian with his glasses and zits.

Even in "Head of the Class," a television show which treats bright, college-bound students with some respect and affection, the students are remarkably unprepossessing. These exceptionally brainy kids are also portrayed as grotesquely fat, thin, hysterical, neurotic, immature, insecure, and the like, compared to the inhabitants of most TV classrooms, who may be dumb but are usually also cool and beautiful.

Such images, of course, have nothing to do with how things turn out in the real world, where top-of-the-class boys and girls frequently end up at the top of professions and sullen dropouts join unemployment lines. But although most of us learn better, we still carry around much stereotyped thinking from our high school days, thinking which influences us more than we may realize. Beside that, the *habits* we form in high school can create powerful blocks when it comes to public speaking.

Double Bind in High School

Remember what it was like, giving reports in front of your tenth grade class? If so, you know the meaning of the term *double bind*.

Let's say the assignment was a book report. Sometime in your fifteen years, you may have actually read a book you liked very much. In fact, you may have liked it so much you read it three times.

But what if you gave an enthusiastic report and said how much you liked it and why? Some of the kids would have laughed at you, wouldn't they? They would have said you were kissing the teacher's . . . shoes. You'd have been humiliated. You may never have lived it down.

Better to talk about this beloved book as if it had bored you out of your skull and you absolutely loathed having to give this stupid report. Still better to report on something you really didn't like at all, so no trace of enthusiasm might sneak through. After all, the purpose of a book report was to mutter and mumble through it as fast as possible, in an anguish of embarrassment, and bore the class to desperation.

This *was* school, after all. The class *expected* to be bored. It *wanted* to be bored. Anything else would not have been cool.

If this was all the training you ever got in public speaking, no wonder it never became your favorite indoor sport.

Getting Rid of Imaginary Audiences

You are a grown-up now. A person with a profession or a business career. You are not planning your presentation for your kindergarten teacher, your mother, your lover, the *New York Review of Books*, or the kids in your tenth grade class. None of them belong in your audience. Time to get them out.

Exorcism #2—That Was Then, This Is Now

Imagine your audience before you. Who *specifically* would you *not* want to be there?

_____ my mother

_____ my father

_____ my sister

_____ my brother

_____ my husband

_____ my wife

_____ my child

_____ my clergyman

_____ my boss

_____ my neighbor

_____ my high school teacher

_____ my college professor

_____ my friends in high school

_____ the ones who weren't my friends in high school

_____ some significant other

Why wouldn't you want them there?

_____

_____

_____

How would they behave? What would they say?_____

_____

_____

_____

How would you feel?

_____

_____

_____

_____

Is this realistic?

_____

Is their opinion relevant to your present situation?

_____

_____

Will you escort them out, the way Moira escorted out her father?

_____

Will you keep doing this until you can do it easily and naturally?

_____

Feel better with them gone?

_____

Do you have a "Supreme Court" judging you?

_____

If so, who is on it?

_____

_____

_____

Who appointed them and why?

_____

_____

_____

What would they say of your performance?

_____

_____

_____

Would you agree with them?

_____

_____

_____

Is this realistic?

_____

_____

_____

Is their opinion relevant to your present situation?

_____

_____

Will you escort them out, the way Moira did her father?

_____

Feel better with them gone?

_____

Imagine your high school English class in your audience.
How would they behave? What would they say?

_____

_____

_____

Would you agree with them?

_____

Is this realistic?

_____

_____

Is their opinion relevant to your present situation?

_____

Will you escort them out too?

_____

Will you feel better with them gone?

_____

Good. No one belongs in your venue but your audience and you.

CLARIFYING AGENDAS

SIMPLIFY! SIMPLIFY! SIMPLIFY!

—*Henry David Thoreau*

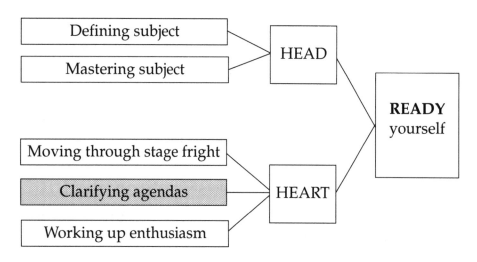

No one has ever gotten up to speak without a complex agenda or motives. Just as there are all these imagined audiences standing between you and the actual one, there are also hidden and fantastic agendas that prevent you from dealing with your immediate purpose.

Open Agendas

Your open or official agenda is the practical goal you intend to achieve, your stated purpose, which is always to pass on something of value to your audience. For example, there may be an organization that has brought you and your listeners together for a particular cause, for you to enlighten them on anything from local politics to cattle breeding to international finance to Japanese films. That organization, and your audience, will expect you to provide pertinent and useful ideas on that particular subject, and perhaps to inspire them to action. Expect no less of yourself.

That organization and your audience will also help you make your presentation as interesting as possible. That too should be part of the goal you intend to achieve.

Hidden Agendas

Aside from such official intentions, there may be other purposes, self-serving purposes, less open even when they are perfectly legitimate.

Perhaps you agreed to this presentation in hopes of getting a raise. Or a promotion. Or of making a commission. Or drumming up future business. Or networking with others in your field. Or being nominated for some office. Or impressing your boss.

These are reasonable motives. Few people have ever made a presentation without having personal goals of this sort in mind.

There may also be ego rewards: the pleasure of showing off what you know and impressing your audience. The adrenaline high you get from being in front of a crowd. The thrill of feeling in control. The greater thrill of skating on the edge and risking the loss of that control.

These too are perfectly legitimate motives. All really good performers share them. They are what gives you the spark that will strike fire in your audience.

But none of these hidden agendas belong in your mind while you are giving your presentation. Remember that your purpose is to communicate something of value to your audience, not to promote yourself. Paradoxically, when you succeed in communicating something of value, personal rewards will surely follow.

Fantastic Agendas

Beyond these rational motives, there may also be, deep within you, wild, secret hopes that have little or nothing to do with your official purpose at all. You may come to this presentation hoping to be discovered and made a media star. Or to meet the love of your life, or someone who will offer you vast sums in exchange for your incomparable talents.

Learn to identify your various agendas and clarify which is which.

Pre-Presentation Agenda Check

Open and Official Agendas

1. _____
2. _____
3. _____

Hidden Agendas

1. _____
2. _____
3. _____
4. _____
5. _____

Fantastic Agendas

1. _____
2. _____
3. _____
4. _____

Just as you must learn to separate the audience in your head from the one in front of your face, you must also find ways to prevent your hidden and fantastic agendas from contaminating your true purpose. Future hopes, like past fears, are out of place in the middle of any task. Forget about your raise or whether there's a potential lover in the house. Such thoughts will only get in your way.

WORKING UP ENTHUSIASM

IN THE CONDITIONS OF MODERN LIFE THE RULE IS
ABSOLUTE, THE RACE WHICH DOES NOT VALUE
TRAINED INTELLIGENCE IS DOOMED.

—Alfred North Whitehead

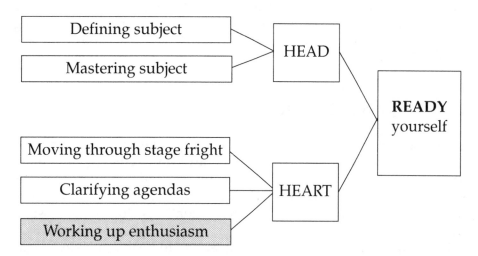

Knowledge and clarity about your subject and an ability to get up and speak are prerequisites of success. There is no way you can give a presentation without them. But they are not enough. Unless you can bring to your presentation a contagiously positive and enthusiastic attitude, you are still nowhere.

Attitude Is Everything

What makes attitude so important? The fact that it is contagious. Research shows that only about seven percent of what we communicate is done through words. The rest is a matter of tone, eyes, and body language.

And what all these express is attitude.

Think of how this works in acting. When actors appear on the stage, screen, or television, we respond at once to how they *look*—before they've had a chance to say a word. We decide on the ones to like and the ones to fear on the basis of their gestures. It's not necessarily a matter of beauty. Plain types like Gene Hackman or Meryl Streep can touch us more than any number of Greek Gods or Sex Queens. They convince us of the reality of their characters by being convinced themselves.

In everyday life it works much the same. First impressions are notoriously powerful and frequently confirmed. People fall in love at first sight or decide there is no way on earth they could ever get along. Addicts and pushers are magnetically attracted to each other. So are bullies and victims, alcoholics and co-dependents, con artists and suckers, rich old men and greedy young women.

Such pairs are said to be reacting to *signals*. That is, one attitude is responding to another. This doesn't just happen with unusual or neurotic types. It happens with all of us, all the time.

You go in for an interview and know in the first instant that you won't get the job. One of you doesn't like the other and the feeling is instantly mutual. You meet a friend for lunch and know at a glance that something is wrong. Will you be able to cheer the friend up, or will the friend drag you down? Two people can't sit at the same table for an hour with two totally different attitudes.

How It Applies to Presentations

As the speaker, you are in charge of the room. All else being equal, it is your attitude that will determine the attitude of your audience. Of course, if they are drunk, or exhausted from ten other speeches, or worried about how to get home in a raging blizzard, your impact will be reduced. Fortunately, most business presentations don't take place under such extreme circumstances.

Most of the time, people will have gathered to hear you because you have information that matters to them. Most of the time, they will have at least some awareness of the importance of that information. They may be wary. If you are a salesperson, for example, they may be on guard against buying from you before they explore alternatives. But at least they have enough at stake to listen.

In our age of information, having relevant information to share is of immense usefulness. Alfred North Whitehead's warning about the failure to value trained intelligence proves its truth more obviously every year. Those who use information well flourish and those who don't fall behind. This is especially true in business, where each year brings more skilled competitors from all over the world.

If you have valuable information to share, then you really have something to be enthusiastic about. You have a great and powerful gift to bestow. You don't have to be an actor. You don't have to play a part. You are Santa Claus. Get excited.

Of course, no one expects you to jump up and down and wave your hands like a five-year-old. But there are other ways to show excitement. Feel it yourself, and your contagious enthusiasm will express itself in your eyes, your voice, your gestures. If *you* believe in the value of what you are saying, then your audience will too. Remember, they are not there to hear *you*, but your *message*.

This is the reason it is so important to put your personal agendas aside and concentrate on your primary purpose. It is there that the benefit to your audience lies. Get excited about what you have to offer, and you will forget about yourself. Let the power of knowledge fill you. That is what you have been preparing for.

When You Choose Your Own Topic

Who chooses your topics for you? Yourself? Your supervisor? An events chairperson?

Whichever it is, make it work for you.

When you are asked to address a club or a convention, speak at a commencement, or give a guest lecture, you are reasonably free to choose your own topic. In that case, the primary rule to remember is to choose from passion.

An odd idea? It shouldn't be.

Choosing from passion does not mean coming from anger or controversy. It means finding a topic that means something important to you and getting that importance across. It's true that some people can't tell the difference. We've all sat through lectures in which we've felt we were being harangued, and they were never pleasant. But avoiding passion means choosing topics that are either obvious or safe and telling your hearers little more than what they already know. They can be a great waste of time.

You may be reluctant to speak from passion for some of these reasons:

- You may be wary of committing yourself.
- You may want to avoid embarrassment.
- You may fear looking unprofessional.
- You may wish to avoid controversy.
- You may dread being faced with hostility.
- You may be afraid to offend.

These are genuine considerations. No one wants to look ridiculous or alienate people. But boring them does both.

If your audience consists of people whose time is worth an average of $50 an hour, and you spend an hour with a hundred of them, telling them nothing new, you have wasted $5000 worth of time. And this does not count the time they lose coming and going, which may be hours more. For those whose time is worth $100 or $500 an hour, the waste becomes all the more shocking.

Lack of confidence in yourself tends to narrow the range of what you care to discuss. You may feel that whole areas are above your head or beyond your horizons. Or that what interests you must be insignificant to others.

There is no such thing as an uninteresting subject. Speakers fired by a passionate interest forget themselves in their excitement. They forge ahead, drawing on inner resources they never knew they had, and carry others away with them.

In the late thirties, two newly dry alcoholics, long-time denizens of drunk tanks, hospitals, and bankruptcy courts, started lecturing other drinkers on how to quit. The result was the foundation of Alcoholics Anonymous and the salvation of countless thousands of lives.

A generation or so later, the parents of a hemophiliac boy became obsessed with the last tsar and tsarina of Russia, whose only son was also a hemophiliac. The result was an international best-seller, *Nicholas and Alexandra*, and important advancements in hemophiliac awareness and care.

More recently, an obscure housewife, whose child was run over and killed, woke up the world by founding MADD (Mothers Against Drunk Drivers). She inspired a national movement and influenced widespread legislation through her speeches.

Still more recently, after losing her baby in a famous custody case, a surrogate mother became an impassioned public speaker, addressing legislative bodies. The result was improved laws regulating surrogacy.

Before these inspired people stepped forth, very few "cared" about skid row alcoholics, drunk drivers, hemophiliac princes, or surrogate mothers. But because excitement is contagious, millions learned to care.

> *If you choose your own topic, the rule is simple:*
> *To be interesting, you must be interested.*
> *To be exciting, you must be excited.*
> *Enthusiasm is all.*
> *So talk about what you care about.*

When Others Choose Your Topic for You

But what if you cannot choose your own subject? What if the choice is up to someone else?

In this case, the advantage is that you are spared the decision. Your task becomes one of searching through the assigned topic to find something that strikes fire in you.

Areas of Overlap

To break through any negative attitudes, look again, both at your own personal interests and the subject of your presentation. What you are looking for are areas of overlap.

With in-house presentations, the reason for your interest tends to be obvious. If you have been working on a project, then you are almost certain to have an emotional interest in its outcome. If you have solved a problem, you will want to share how this has been done. If there is a controversy, you will want to state your side. If you have a goal, you will want to implement it. If you have a need, you will want to do what is required to get it filled. If you have problems still unsolved, it will benefit you to clarify what they are, determine possible steps, and seek for advice or assistance.

Work Through Your Blocks and Work Up an Interest

The secret of growth, both personal and professional, lies in that simple but magical formula.

There is only one exception to that rule. Where you feel a true aversion to an assignment, either redefine it or turn it down.

A True Confession

I once made a fool of myself, by agreeing to give a speech on assertiveness training to a major professional convention. This was anything but a compatible topic, as assertiveness training is largely based on behaviorism, an approach I resist without other supportive therapy.

At first, I was wise enough to refuse. "Look, I'm no expert in assertiveness training. I only speak about things I know about and believe in." But the events chairperson of the conference kept after me, skillfully appealing to my vanity, my ambition and my greed. "Oh, Joan, you're such an enthusiastic speaker. You can talk about anything for an hour. They just want a basic introduction, that's all. Besides, how can you turn down such an opportunity? This will open up a whole new audience for you. Besides, think of the fee! All that money for just one hour's work! And you have three whole months to prepare."

In the end, I caved in. (Actually, I could have done with a little more assertiveness training myself.)

Although I enlarged my knowledge of the subject, nothing I learned fired my enthusiasm. As a result, I gave a lackluster presentation and rather disgraced myself with the events chairperson.

The problem was partly that the subject had been defined too inflexibly. If I could have dealt with my questions about assertiveness training, I would certainly have done better. Since this approach was not permitted, I should have been firm about turning down the offer.

There is a simple lesson to be drawn from this experience. *Know yourself.*

Chapter Two

ON YOUR MARK

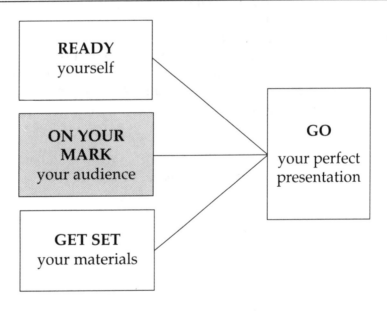

Professor X at the Y

Once upon a time in a major midwestern city (this is no fairy tale), a well-known literary scholar in his forties joined the local YMCA so he could use the swimming pool. One day he was asked if he would be so kind as to speak about poetry to the Y's senior citizen verse-writing class. The scholar generously agreed, and devoted a full hour to lecturing an audience of eighty-year-olds on his specialty, the relationship between the Pan-Slavic movement and Romantic poetry in nineteenth-century Russia. Needless to say, by the time he was done, there was hardly an open eye in the room.

For all his years of teaching, his publications and his Ph.D., Professor X had somehow never learned the First Rule of Public Speaking:

Always tailor your presentation to your audience.

A Joint Venture with Your Audience

There are presenters who mistakenly think only of pleasing the listener— whether it be the boss, a client, a committee, or an audience. Alas, people who try too hard to please seldom do. This is as true in public life as it is in private life.

Others think only of pleasing themselves—continuing on automatic pilot with little awareness of how they are going over. The result is inevitably a variation on the theme of Professor X.

Good presenters know that they are involved in a duet, a joint venture, a dance. They realize that the success of any such partnership can be measured only by how well it works for both parties. There is no way you can be satisfied unless your audience is. And there is no way your audience can enjoy itself unless you do.

Like you, your listeners have their private histories and hidden and fantastic agendas. Like you, they are former children. Like you, they are conditioned by the past, busy with the present, and concerned about the future. Many of them have given presentations of their own, just as you have often sat among them to listen.

In other words, they are people just like you. They are not a Supreme Court, unless you choose to make them one.

So begin by imagining yourself a part of your own audience. What kind of presentation would motivate, teach, or inspire *you?*

Audience Profile

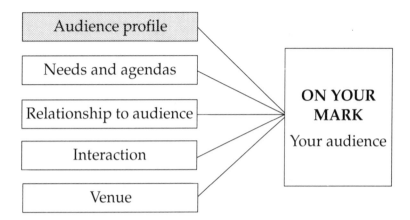

Despite their common humanity, different audiences have different needs and require different approaches. Your audience needs just as much thinking about as the things you are going to say. A real estate agent faced with a client, a preacher in front of his congregation, or a chairman meeting with the board, would all look ridiculous using each other's delivery. Imagine the chairman exhorting like a preacher, or the preacher trying to close like a salesman.

Even within your own company, your tone will differ depending on whether you are reporting to a superior, a subordinate, or a peer. Or whether you are addressing one person, twenty, or two hundred. Or whether you are dealing with experts in your field or novices.

Nothing is more crucial to the success of your presentation than to make an audience profile. Everything to come in this chapter deals with some aspect of audience profiling, but let's begin with a broad overview.

Audience Profile Questionnaire

Who will be attending my presentation? Where are they from? _____

_____

What will be their main purpose in being there? _____

_____

_____

Will they also be there to (check as many as apply)

  Keep their jobs? _____

  Get promoted? _____

  Be entertained? _____

  Improve their finances? _____

Deal with a personal problem? ____

Network or meet people? ____

Are they also specifically

Interested in me? ____

Interested in my subject? ____

Any other factors? _____

_____

_____

How will I adapt to their expectations? _____

_____

_____

Will they be attending voluntarily, or on somebody's orders? _____

About how many will there be? _____

Is this an internal or a public presentation? _____

If internal, will my listeners be mainly subordinates, superiors, or peers?

_____

In what proportions? _____

What will be the setting?

Auditorium? __

Conference hall? ____

Meeting room? ____

Theater? ____

TV studio? ____

My office? ____

Their office? ____

My home? ____

Their home? ____

Other? _____

How can I adapt to these factors? _____

_____

_____

_____

What is their likely age range? _____

Educational level? _____

Ethnic composition? _____

Professional composition? _____

Class or social status? _____

Level of competence? _____

Personal involvement? _____

How will I adapt to these characteristics? _____

_____

_____

_____

What immediate use will they make of what I tell them?

_____

What long-term use? _____

_____

How much specific knowledge can I expect them to have about the subject?

_____

_____

Will their level of knowledge be consistent, or will it vary significantly?

_____

_____

How can I adapt to these conditions? _____

_____

_____

_____

_____

An effective opening sentence for such an audience would be: _____

_____

_____

_____

An effective close would be: _____

_____

_____

_____

NEEDS AND AGENDAS

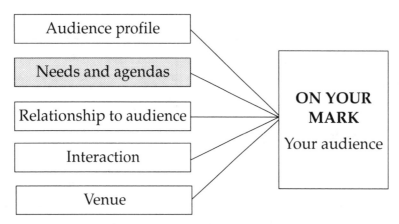

Before you can serve your listener's needs and agendas, you have to find out what they are. The best way to start is with three comparatively simple questions and one somewhat tougher one.

Three Simple Questions

How are things for my audience now, before I give my presentation?

_____

_____

_____

_____

What change will my presentation make? _____

_____

_____

_____

How will they benefit? _____

_____

_____

_____

_____

Once you have your answers, the next step is to put them into a category. This idea will seem anything but appealing. Your whole soul may rebel against the sin of pigeonholing.

Do it anyway. Choose one answer and one only.

One Tougher Question

Is my primary purpose to:

1. Solve a problem? _____
2. Argue an opinion? _____
3. Prove a thesis? _____
4. Give instructions? _____
5. Pass along information? _____

Now take a breath. Relax. We're almost there—but not quite. In the words of the immortal Columbo, "Begging your pardon, sir [or madam]. There's just one more thing."

Let's assume that your presentation accomplished all you intend it to do. Let's also assume it's exactly what your audience needs to hear. How would you summarize the intended result, in *terms of the primary purpose you have just chosen?*

In other words, how would you now define your official agenda—and theirs?

Official Agenda Summary

(choose one)

My audience will now be able to identify, define, and solve a particular *problem.* _____ That problem is:

_____

_____

My audience will now have seen sufficient evidence to prove my *thesis.* _____ That thesis is: _____

_____

_____

My audience will now have adequate *instructions* to do something they couldn't do before. _____ They will know how to: _____

_____

My audience will now have *information* they didn't have before. _____ This information concerns: _____

_____

_____

Secret and Hidden Agendas

Few people are so single-minded as to have only an official agenda. Like you, your audience will have hidden and irrational ones as well. These could be anything from impressing a boss to getting a day away from the desk to gorging on the goodies. A few may even be hoping that you will supply them with some Secret of the Universe that will change the entire course of their lives.

One thing is certain. These secondary agendas will exist and they will be a distraction. You need not pander to them, but you ignore them at your peril.

Whenever possible, adjust your subject matter, your tone, and the length of your speech to the probable interest level and attention span of your audience. If you must lure them from one frame of mind to another, begin where they are likely to be. For example, if you wish to address celebrating conventioneers on a serious subject, begin lightly, amusingly, then gradually veer in the direction you want them to go.

RELATIONSHIP TO AUDIENCE

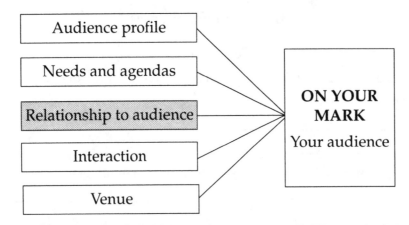

Eight key questions will help define your relationship to your listeners.

The Eight Key Questions

1. How large is your audience?
2. Are they internal to your company or external?
3. Are they captive or voluntary?
4. Are they expert, inexpert, or mixed?
5. Are they superiors, subordinates, or peers?
6. Are you selling them something?

7. Are they on their turf, yours, or neutral ground?
8. Are you giving them good news or bad?

1. The Size of Your Audience

One listener? Fifty? Or a thousand? No variable matters more. For many speakers, the larger the audience, the greater the dread. And yet, as a rule, the larger the audience, the more passive each listener, and the less likely to challenge the speaker.

When you address an audience of a thousand, you are in control. Once you have planned what to say, your head-work is done. Crutches are permitted. Few will be shocked if you rely on rote memory, notes, or even a written script. And most probably no one will be able to back you into a corner with unwelcome questions.

With fifty, or twenty, it becomes more awkward to use such crutches. With under ten, it is impossible. You can't lecture one person from a frozen script or refuse to answer his questions.

The smaller the number, the more responsive you'll have to be. This requires in-depth knowledge. Many salespeople are trained to recite a script and to give rote replies to common objections. But some prospects won't play their role. When this happens, good salespersons must dump their scripts and rely on themselves: their knowledge of the product, their ability to improvise, and their willingness to engage the prospect in a sensitive, individual way.

Those same abilities are needed when you give presentations within your organization, especially to superiors, and to small numbers. There's no way you can read to three people, or even use a lot of notes. You would look simply incompetent. You can't rely on rote memorization either, since you are sure to be asked to skip some of what you've memorized and deal with matters you haven't. You're also sure to be questioned, sometimes mercilessly. You have to know your stuff and be able to think on your feet.

2. External and Internal Presentations

Negotiation theorists have taught us the difference between negotiating with one-deal partners, such as someone buying your house, and with long-term partners, such as clients you hope to keep forever. With the one-deal partner, you bargain for the best terms you can get. With the long-term partner, you settle for less and concede more, to keep the partnership going.

External presentations are like negotiating with one-deal partners. You "go for it" to the max. You strive to stand out, to outperform your competition, whether it be in getting the listing or stealing the show. External presentations tend to be relatively formal, ritualized occasions.

They also require you to supply more background, to give more explanations.

Internal presentations are for long-term associates, people who are familiar with you and what you are attempting. They tend to be somewhat informal, intimate occasions. They aim at agreed-upon results, and take a common frame of reference for granted.

The concepts of *external* and *internal* apply also to presentations for special interest groups. Addresses by Masons to Masons, by Baptists to Baptists, by Democrats to Democrats, all constitute *internal* presentations. Speaker and audience share a common agenda and purpose. Consider the direct, informal tone of Sheila Murray Bethel, author of *Making a Difference*, as she addresses her fellow professional speakers at a convention:

> *You don't want to be this little automaton that comes on stage and clicks on the switch and becomes this other thing. The most important thing with credibility is you must connect with people, and if you're this false image, you won't connect. You've got to get the barriers down. You've got to be real with people.*

3. Captive and Voluntary Audiences

There are four degrees of audience willingness.

Captive audiences are those literally forced to attend. Prison inmates or draftees have no say about being called to assembly. Those who address them are seldom motivated to please.

You are not likely to be giving presentations to totally captive audiences.

Virtually captive audiences have somewhat more choice, but it's mainly theoretical. Middle managers sick to death of committee meetings are technically free to walk out, even to quit their jobs. But how often do they do it?

With virtually captive audiences, your task is to arouse their latent interest, to raise their low expectations, and to infect them with your own enthusiasm.

Semivoluntary audiences are there because they want to be, more or less. Employees might take an offered seminar because it breaks their routine, although they'd really rather go to the beach. Conventioneers will genially tolerate the speeches, although the speeches were hardly the prime attraction.

Semivoluntary audiences are easy to please. They are in a mind-set to benefit and enjoy, but their expectations are not excessive.

Voluntary audiences are exactly where they most want to be. They can't wait to hear the famous author or favorite candidate, learn more about their profession or hobby, solve some urgent problem, or participate in their own growth.

Voluntary audiences offer the greatest opportunities for triumphant success or abysmal failure. They expect something very special. Deliver it, and you may get an ovation. Disappoint them, and they won't hesitate to let you know.

4. Expert, Inexpert, and Mixed Audiences

You and your audience may be at very different levels of sophistication and knowledge. Call it the *Professor X factor*. Unless you gauge it accurately, you risk insulting the knowledgeable and baffling the ignorant. It would seem obvious that computer specialists don't need to hear what *bytes* and *bits* are, but word-processing novices ought to be told. The Professor X factor is all about common sense, yet an astonishing number of speakers seem oblivious to it.

Expert audiences expect you to be an expert too. Their time is valuable, so they hate to waste it. If you have any doubts about yourself, facing experts can be an ordeal.

You stand your best chance for success if you follow two guidelines:

1. *Be as head-ready as possible.* Master your subject. Have such in-depth knowledge that you will scarcely have time to skim off the cream.

2. *Honor their expertise.* Never waste their valuable time or offend them by harping on common knowledge. Get to the point. Be thorough but economical. Concentrate on the freshest information, the most useful applications.

With *inexpert audiences*, you are the expert. They can't judge your content, only your delivery. Keep their goodwill, and you will find them easy to handle. You can do this if you follow two rules:

1. *Be enthusiastic.* Deliberately pique and stir up their interest. Guide them to appreciate the significance and value of their subject. Assume they will be excited to learn.

2. *Take nothing for granted.* Slighting the fundamentals is one of the marks of poor teaching. Don't be embarrassed to start from ground zero. If you are introducing a new piece of equipment, begin by showing them where the on-off switch is. Make a joke about it, but don't skip it. Keep communication open. Make sure you don't leave them behind.

Mixed audiences are the hardest to plan for. How do you discuss commodities, for example, when some of your audience has been investing in them for decades, while others aren't even sure what a commodity is?

Actually, mixed audiences can be a joy, so long as you remember two simple ideas:

1. *Begin with a review of the fundamentals.* Keep your language simple and free from jargon, and define basic terms as you go. All this will orient the novices. At the same time, spice up this opening review with original ideas and examples. These will alert the more expert that you have something fresh to say.

2. *Rely heavily on stories and examples.* Use them to emphasize general trends and principles, rather than figures and details. Even a relatively specialized subject, such as corporation management or demographic trends, can be made accessible to a mixed audience. Just avoid heavily technical language and give plenty of examples and illustrations.

5. Superiors, Subordinates, and Peers

Most organizations are class systems, complete with codes of behavior and etiquette that everyone soon learns and takes for granted. For example, in most companies you await your superior's convenience and expect your own subordinates to do the same for you. Ways of doing things may differ in small ways from company to company, but the basic rules are the same.

When you make a presentation for superiors, you tailor your work to their specifications. Likely as not, your topic will have been preassigned or preapproved. Many of the same factors apply as when you make a presentation for experts.

When you make a presentation for subordinates, you tend to choose your own subject, based on judgment of what they need to know. It's rather like being the expert, facing an inexpert audience.

When you present to peers, your subject has usually evolved from previous discussions. You have all decided together what everyone needs to know. Since your peers may differ in their areas of expertise, you use some of the same tactful approach you would take with mixed audiences.

6. If You're Selling Something

Sales presentations all follow a basic structure. Whether you are in a living room selling an insurance policy, or in a boardroom promoting a computer system, your presentation will employ the same structured format:

1. Establish rapport.
2. Awaken the listener to a need, problem, or desire.
3. Show how your product or service can satisfy it.
4. Answer questions and counter objections.

5. Establish or reinforce urgency.
6. Ask for the order.

Many companies provide their sales force with scripts, in which these steps are codified. All memorize and rehearse the same scripts. Most are personable and also motivated. Yet some will succeed and others will not. The difference between success and lack of it depends mainly on three factors:

1. How able salespersons are to rely on the structure rather than the script
2. How well they profile their prospects
3. How flexibly they respond to prospects' cues

Actually, there is not much difference between sales presentations and every other kind. Each time you apply for a job, teach something from a platform, or discuss a public issue, you are trying to sell *something*—yourself or your ideas. It should not be surprising that you will be following the same basic structure:

1. Establish rapport.
2. Arouse an interest in yourself or your subject.
3. Show how it will be useful or beneficial to your audience.
4. Respond to (or anticipate) their questions.
5. Leave mutually satisfied.

If you are selling yourself, a product, or a service, the mutually satisfactory conclusion will be an order or a contract. If you are selling information or ideas, the mutually satisfactory conclusion will be your audience's sense that they have learned something of value, and your own gratification for having provided it.

7. Their Turf, Yours, or Neutral Ground

As any bullfight aficionado knows, the first thing a bull does when loosed into the ring is to choose his *querencia*. Some spot to call home. In a word, his turf.

There he will return any time he feels threatened, or hurt, or wishes to gather his resources. A matador who cannot lure him out is in big trouble.

Human beings also have *querencias*. Ball teams win more games at home than on the road. Executives feel most powerful behind their own desks.

Doctors and lawyers expect you to come to them instead of going to you—unless you are a high-ranking tycoon or celebrity.

People in sales have a gut-level awareness of what turf can mean. Going to other people's homes and offices, they must prepare for rudeness and rejection. If they are to survive in the profession, they must learn not to take it personally. The best of them learn to play a kind of mental judo, turning the other person's strength to their own benefit. Skilled salespersons, for example, can inveigle their clients into perceiving them as guests rather than intruders. It then works to their advantage to be on the other person's turf.

Awareness is power. Unless you are very high in the hierarchy indeed, you will often be presenting someone else's *querencia*. Like the salesperson, you must learn to turn that disadvantage into an advantage.

For some successful speakers, their very status as the presenter becomes a kind of portable *querencia*. They learn to feel stronger up front than mingling with the audience during breaks. Some who are desperately shy in private life become brilliant presenters, drawing their strength from being the one in control.

8. Good or Bad News

Good news is always a delight to deliver. Mixed news is a normal and expected fact of life. But sometimes you must get up to say things that will cause serious pain. There is no easy way to tell people that layoffs are coming, or that the quarterly report is a disaster, or that a death or accident has occurred.

The best way is to say what must be said as simply and directly as possible, without diluting your message or mixing it with other news. Call your meeting for the specific purpose, express your regret, give your news, and then, whenever possible, discuss how the problem might be mitigated or redefined. In most cases, it would be in bad taste to warm up your audience with humor or to mix this news with more trivial matters.

A Warning About Flypaper—the Introductory Speech

There is one kind of speech we have yet to consider: the introduction of a speaker. No other kind of presentation is butchered so often. Antiquated formalities, obsolete flatteries, and silly clichés stick to introductions like flies to flypaper. *And now, it is my honor to present . . . a man who . . . a man who . . . a man who . . . needs no introduction . . . And so now, without further ado . . . I turn the microphone over to our most celebrated and honored guest, the distinguished and . . . et cetera, et cetera, et cetera.*

Sometimes, of course, introducers will lean too far the other way: *You all know George Smith. He's the bald guy who just walked in late. Stopped off for a bit of action, did you, George? Sorry, just kidding. Anyway, Georgie's going to talk about something important. How he got out of that embezzlement indictment, ha ha! Come on up here, you sonofagun. That is, if you're not too drunk to stand on your feet.*

It is rare that either the boast or the roast makes an appropriate introduction. Both are self-conscious extremes, the product of embarrassment. Ours is a *Hey, Joe, meet Bob* society. Formal introductions are done so rarely that we don't know how to make them, except by falling back on the language and tone of another time. When that seems impossible, we seem to have no recourse but sick humor.

To make an appropriate introduction, keep things simple. Your language should be gracious and reasonably traditional, but not trite, pompous, or antique. Your format should be to the point, flattering but not fawning, representative but not exhaustive. Your purpose, after all, is to explain to the audience who this person is and why he or she is worth listening to. It's not to narrate the person's biography, bury him in compliments, or draw attention to yourself.

Some speakers prefer to write their own introductions and hand them to the introducer. This is perfectly reasonable. Speakers have the right to control what is said of them and what is not. If asked to read a speaker's self-introduction, do so as it is written, but look it over first to get fluent and be comfortable. Of course, omit anything that might offend.

Structure for an Introduction

Identify yourself and your position.

Good afternoon. I'm Dalton Miller, your events committee chairperson.

Explain that you're introducing the speaker and who the speaker is.

It's my privilege this afternoon to introduce our guest speaker, Dr. Helen Otis. Dr. Otis is a professor of industrial psychology at Ivy University and author of numerous articles and books, including the classic text in the field, The Psychology of the Workplace.

Expand briefly on the most relevant aspect of the speaker's credentials.

Dr. Otis has recently been studying the psychological implications of retraining manual workers for service positions, a subject of crucial interest here at XYZ. She will be sharing her latest findings with us here today.

Give some idea of the structure of the presentation.

Dr. Otis will discuss her research for about thirty minutes, then answer questions for the rest of the hour.

Complete the introduction, shake hands with the speaker, and step aside.

I ask you to join me now in welcoming Dr. Helen Otis.

Last Words

It should go without saying, but it's best to say it anyway: Nothing should be said from any business podium that is offensive or demeaning to others, particularly on the grounds of race, ancestry, religion, national origin, sexual identity, or the like.

INTERACTION

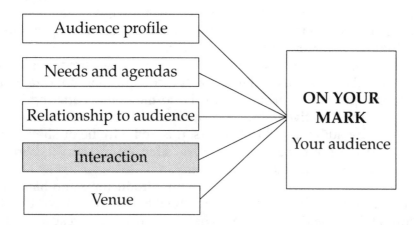

Nothing is more important than monitoring the mood of your audience and making a shift in style when your presentation isn't working.

I once gave a presentation on "How to Remember Names" for a group of securities analysts. We had not gone ten minutes before I realized that I was bombing. I was truly baffled. This opening had always worked. What was going on?

The answer came in a flash. I always began with exercises that related memory to feelings. It appeared this didn't work with securities analysts, at least with these securities analysts. I decided to skip over the emotional material and go directly to "logical stuff" like mnemonics. My audience perked right up and the rest of the presentation went beautifully.

Another time, I was giving a presentation seminar at a major corporation, and getting little response. Nothing I tried made any difference, and I could not think of anything about the audience I had not taken into consideration.

I finally asked what was wrong and I discovered it had nothing to do with me. Cutbacks had been announced only that morning and my listeners were distracted with worries about getting laid off. Once the air was cleared, however, we reasoned that wherever they might be working in the future, they could use better speaking skills. From that point on, the session went well.

When Things Go Flat

Audiences always let you know how you are doing, so keep your eyes and ears open. Notice if they are restless or trying to fill time with something else. If one or two out of fifty are whispering or nodding off, it might not mean too much. They may have their own personal reasons. But if several act that way, do something. Ask, "Is this helpful so far?" or something of the sort.

What is going on between you and these people? Could it be that the audience you anticipated is not identical with the one that showed up? Is it much smaller or larger, or sorted differently as to age, sex, education, or ethnic mix? What are you doing that might be wrong for this particular group?

Changing Your Approach

Try to pinpoint the problem. Could it be:

1. *Your tone?* Are you trying to pump up a somber bunch with too much playfulness? Or are you too serious for this lively crowd? Are you being too formal for a small group or too casual for a large one?

2. *Your subject?* Have you come to speak on something too difficult (or possibly too easy)? Are you too far above (or below) their level?

3. *Your focus?* Is the subject all right, but the angle or approach unsuitable?

4. *Your attitude?* Do you lack energy or enthusiasm? (Remember that emotion is contagious.)

Livening It Up

To give an immediate lift to almost any flagging presentation, you have three major resources:

1. *Your own experiences.* Things that have happened to *you* have an authentic feel that stirs audience identification. Use an example. Tell how you solved a similar problem, as I did with the securities analysts.

2. *Other people's experiences.* One picture, they say, is worth a thousand words, and certain stories create indelible pictures. So make plentiful use of real-life stories. But if there is even the smallest chance that what you tell might invade anyone's privacy, be sure to disguise the names and circumstances. If you should borrow an example from someone else's speech or a published work, always give credit. "X used to tell the story about . . ."

3. *Humor.* Lightening up and seeing the funny side helps to relax any audience. If you're good at it, you might tell jokes, but only if you're good at it. Patricia Fripp, past president of the National Speakers As-

sociation, said it best: *"You may ask, 'Do I have to be funny?' I ask you. 'Are you funny? If you're not funny, be inspiring.'"*

Become a Collector

Supply yourself with the stories, anecdotes, and amusing tales you will need, by gathering them as you go through life. Collect them from what you see, hear, and read. Jot them on index cards and file them under suitable headings. Work some into every presentation, and keep more in reserve.

Facts, Figures, and Authorities

To give weight and substance to your presentation, make use *(but very cautious use)* of two further resources:

1. *Statistics and data.* Specific facts add credibility, but don't overdo them. They are not easily followed or retained by the ear. Visual information such as charts and graphs convey data with far more effectiveness than words can do. Use them. Go easy on dates. If you must use many figures, round them off whenever possible.

2. *References to authority.* Allusions to experts indicate that you know your field. Vivid and appropriate quotations help support your position. Like facts and figures, however, these should not be overdone. There's not much point quoting when you can express an idea just as neatly yourself. And constant name-dropping shows a lack of confidence in your own value.

Dealing with Hostility

Antagonism from your audience can ruin a presentation, unless it is properly handled. In his excellent book, *Spokesperson*, Ken W. Huskey makes several valuable suggestions for deflecting the worst of it. His advice is directed to people active in politics and social issues, but certain aspects of it can be used by anyone.

For example, when you anticipate hostility, you can establish ground rules in advance. You can tell them how long you will speak and how much time you will give them for questions. You can ask questioners to identify themselves before asking and then to relinquish the microphone as soon as you begin your reply. You can have an assistant who takes the microphone away. You can even ask for all questions to be written out in advance.

Under most circumstances, you will not have these options. You will have to deal with hostilities as they occur. Most abusive behavior will pass in reasonable time if you follow a few simple guidelines:

1. Stay cool. Don't lose your temper or answer in kind.
2. Hear your critic out. Thank him for expressing his opinion.
3. If appropriate, reply briefly and politely.
4. If you prefer, simply resume your presentation or take the next question.
5. Humor (but not gross sarcasm) can be helpful.

There is the true story of the CEO of a major corporation who was verbally assailed while speaking at a university. When the disrupter finally shut up, the CEO smiled and said, "Thank you for your frankness. You can trust me to keep it off the record." The responsive laughter immediately broke the tension.

Circumstances Beyond Your Control

Once in a while, audiences will fail to respond for reasons that have little to do with you. Like the seminar group worried about layoffs, they may be distracted by extraneous factors. There's an old saying that you should never mention rope in a household where someone has just been hanged. But you don't always know someone has been hanged.

So don't neglect to ask. Inviting people to speak up creates trust and intimacy. You may well learn something crucial about your audience. Or even about yourself.

Treating Their Time as Valuable

Above all, don't waste their time. Patrica Fripp describes a typical occasion:

We had a speaker for our sales and marketing executives' club in San Francisco. He had an hour to talk, was twenty minutes late in starting ("beyond his control"), but he had to finish on time. He started out by saying how nice it was to be in San Francisco, how great the weather was, how much better than in Washington, D.C., which he had just left, how he loved the restaurants. *Who cares?!?* I did not race across town and bring my administrator to hear him talk about weather and restaurants.

VENUE

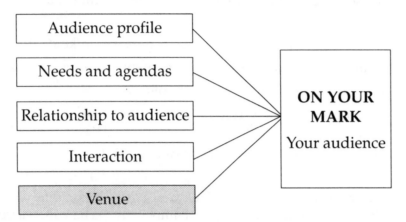

A presentation can take place in all sorts of places, from the cramped dining area of a house trailer to an amphitheater holding thousands. It can be addressed to a single person, face to face, or to hundreds of millions by satellite.

Six Venues for Business Presentations

1. **Sales presentations in homes**
2. **Sales presentations in business settings**
3. **Speeches to service clubs or banquets**
4. **Addresses to conventions or conferences**
5. **Internal reports to superiors**
6. **Internal reports to subordinates and peers**

Several of these we have already considered in other contexts. There is no need to do more than touch on the major points.

Sales presentations in homes take place in the homeowner's *querencia*, or turf. The salesperson's first priority is to establish himself as a guest, win trust, and take whatever control he can. This can be done by requesting things, suggesting credentials, asking questions, and making suggestions. "May I please have a glass of water?" "This is a delightful neighborhood. I was the listing agent when the Brackmans sold the house, you know." "What a beautiful photograph. Lovely little girl. Is she your daughter?" "May I sit right here, so you can both see at once?"

Only then should you get on with your presentation.

Sales presentations in business settings depend on the setting. It's one thing to be chasing an owner-chef around his diner trying to interest him in a better doggie bag, and quite another to be demonstrating communications equipment to ten decision makers at a large corporation.

However, these settings have a good deal in common. Once again, you are on the other guy's turf. You can't make yourself a guest because this is not a home. But you can turn yourself into a kind of colleague. You are people with a common goal—the client's welfare.

Profile the company. If they wear suits and ties and conduct their business formally, meet their standards. If they are casual in dress and manner, let down a little. Take cues from the vocal patterns, body language, and general demeanor that prevail.

Be prepared to adapt your presentation to their equipment. Be prepared to use any sort of audiovisual equipment they may have, and also to do without it.

Speeches in front of service clubs and banquets require you to compete with the meal, the in-house reports, other people's speeches, and the general sociability of the crowd. These may take place in all sorts of places, most commonly restaurants or meeting halls.

Lunch meetings must end on schedule, since people have to get back to work. But at least the audience is wide awake. You can speak on a serious subject, but make sure you can cut the length on short notice.

Dinner meetings go on for several hours. People eat, drink, and relax, and some may be half asleep by the time your turn arrives. Don't demand too much of them. This is no time or place for a major address.

Speeches to conventions and conferences are a mixed bag. Your audience will be fellow professionals genuinely interested in you, your work, or your topic. They expect to learn from you and demand a high level of performance. On the other hand, they will be worn out from travel, caught in tight schedules, and easily distracted by the novelty of being in a different and probably very alluring environment. Typically, there will be several presentations going on in succession and also simultaneously, which can mean a messy venue, all sorts of confusion, and no help on hand if anything breaks down.

A few years ago, a well-known biologist was invited to address a major conference in Germany. At the very last minute, he fell ill and sent his junior collaborator. The slides were not quite ready, so the whiz promised to send them air express. After that, it was a Marx Brothers movie, with the slides not arriving and no projector reserved. A projector did finally become available—two hours *after* the presentation. Not that it mattered, since the slides were still wandering around Euorpe and did not arrive until the next day. The novice collaborator sweated and stammered his way through the presentation with no sense of how comic the whole thing was until several days later, while relaxing on a ski slope in Bavaria.

> ## Guidelines for Giving Presentations Far from Home
>
> - Arrive at least a day in advance. If you're going to a foreign country, try to make that two days.
> - Imagine everything that could go wrong and make contingency plans.
> - Carry all dire necessities with you, including electric current converters.
> - Keep things as simple as possible.
> - Check out your venue well in advance.
> - Always carry master copies of any handouts, and find a local quick-copy printer. Your own copies may not arrive in time, or there may not be enough. So prepare yourself to get more made on the spot.
> - Rely on no one but yourself.

Internal reports to superiors take place in the big guy's *querencia*. All you can do is your best. Think in terms of the *Eight Be's:*

The Eight Be's

Be prompt.
Be presentable.
Be prepared.
Be relevant.
Be organized.
Be receptive.
Be thorough.
Be brief.

The Eight Be's can be applied to most presentations. But they are particularly crucial when dealing with upper management. A lonely old widow might be grateful to pass half the day with a friendly salesperson. But every hour of executive time can be worth thousands of dollars to a major organization. If several executives are sitting in to hear you, keep in mind the value of every minute, and make sure they get their money's worth.

Prepare actively for such meetings. Plan for success. Profile your listeners. What can you learn about their interests that you can use to establish rapport? Ask others who have presented reports to them. What has worked? What has not?

When you must give reports to a large internal group, including superiors, subordinates, and peers, be sure to put the needs of the superiors first. You can always catch up with subordinates and peers at a later time.

Internal reports to subordinates and peers ought to be the easiest. The people are almost like family. The venue is almost like home. And that is the problem. Just like your kith and kin, these are the people you feel most free to quarrel with, your most likely spat-partners, annoyances, and rivals.

Don't let familiarity breed contempt or irritation. Try to be as considerate of your peers and subordinates as you would be of your employers or clients.

Pep Talks

One type of internal presentation given to subordinates is the pep talk. These should be both informal and short. Your purpose is to encourage and energize your listeners, not to exhaust them. Humor is also important.

Pep talks are not the proper venue for discussing any individual's shortcomings. Save those for private meetings in your office.

The Cardinal Rule When It Comes to Audiences

Assume that, all else being equal, your audience prefers good times over bad. Good times don't necessarily mean drunken orgies or sessions of stand-up comedy. Any meeting that genuinely stimulates the mind or the spirits can count as a good time.

What makes times good, above all, is a sense of being alive and being excited. Give that to your audience and there is no way your presentation can fail to succeed.

Chapter Three

GET SET

In the beginning was the word, and the word had impact, and so must you . . . Come out punching.

—*Patricia Fripp, Past President,*
National Speakers Association

FOCUSING QUESTIONS

You've worked through the worst of your nerves. You know pretty well what you want to say. You know who's going to be listening and what they need from you.

All you have to do now is to put the presentation together and deliver it.

Is that all? you well may ask.

Yes, that *is* all. And, fortunately it doesn't have to be anywhere near so awesome a task as you suppose.

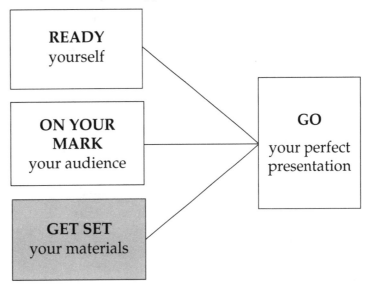

You begin, as usual, by asking yourself some focusing questions—to get you clear on what has already been accomplished, and what is still left to do.

The following exercise will give you a very good start.

Focusing Exercise

How can I summarize my topic in a single sentence?

_____

How can I summarize my major conclusion in a single sentence? ____

_____

What subtopics do I want to cover? How can I summarize each in one short sentence?

(1) _____

(2) _____

(3) _____

Are there any key phrases or definitions that would focus and clarify things?

(1) _____

(2) _____

(3) _____

What information will I need that I don't have? _____

_____

_____

_____

Is it at hand or will I need to do more research? _____

_____

Where can I find this information? _____

_____

_____

Will I use audiovisual materials? _____

What kind? _____

_____

Are they available or will I have to arrange for them?_____

_____

How? From where? From whom? _____

_____

Will I have to learn new skills (like running a projector)? Or get skilled help (such as a projectionist)? Or find muscle power (to carry in heavy objects)? If so, list such needs: _____

_____

_____

_____

RESEARCHING

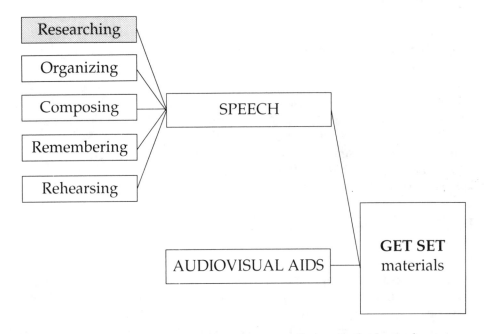

Researching and organizing are two aspects of one single, logical process. You organize as you research, and you research as you organize.

Sometimes, as when you are reporting on your own work-in-progress, virtually all the information you need will be at hand. At other times, you may have to go find it. You will find lists of sources, along with other helpful hints, in an appendix, *Research Source Materials*.

How to Do Your Research

There is no one right way to do research. There is, however, a process, which breaks down into four logical steps:

1. Identify what information you need.
2. Search the appropriate sources.
3. Record the information in a usable form.
4. Organize the information.

To achieve this, some surround themselves with mountains of sources, flipping their way through and finding what they need by serendipity. Others search one item at a time in a systematic way. Some write voluminous marginal notes while others consider any mark in a book as tantamount to rape or desecration.

Do whatever suits you, so long as you are mindful of the goal:

The purpose of research is to locate relevant information and then put it where you can get at it.

Locating Relevant Information

If the nature and structure of your presentation are simple, doing your research usually will be too. You want to report on trends in the PC market? The places to look are easily found.

But what if you're pursuing something broader and less exact, such as trends in corporate employee training? You will want to know so many things. How much corporations are spending. What kind of training they're giving. What kind of results they're getting. To learn all that, you may need to search far and wide. The topic is enormous. You'll either have to limit yourself to generalizations or focus in on certain aspects only.

Putting It Where You Can Find It

Creating access is the crucial step. If you can't use what you have found, it's worthless. Two simple techniques will pay off bounteously. First, as you go through your reading, flag the pages where essential charts, statistics, ideas, or possible quotes are to be found. If you want to make marginal notes, put them on the flags. If your flagged pages are in library volumes that you can't take home, be sure to photocopy the pages with the notes in place.

At the end of each session, or at any other appropriate interval, sift through and decide what you want to keep, then transfer those ideas, quotes, and charts to index cards, putting source information (author, volume, publisher, date, and page number) on the backs. Don't ever handwrite more than a sentence or two. Clipping and gluing photocopied material will save you time now and make for easier deciphering later on.

Old-fashioned and low-tech as this approach may sound, you will soon see that it has enormous advantages.

ORGANIZING

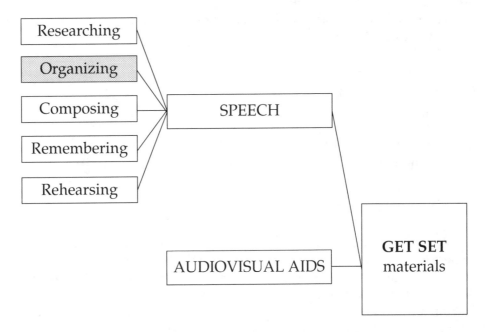

The key to organizing your materials is knowing the kind of speech you intend to give.

Let's look again at the Five Patterns of Organization: Problem, Opinion, Thesis, Instruction, and Information. This time, we will consider them more closely, one by one.

Problem Pattern

This is the pattern to use when dealing with something that has gone wrong and needs correcting.

Example: We're not attracting the quality sales force we need. Why not? And what can we do about it?

Your presentation should:

- State the problem.
- Demonstrate the effects.
- Trace the causes.
- Offer solutions.
- Summarize.

Opinion Pattern

This is the pattern to use with an idea that cannot be put to the proof before you commit to it—such as a political, religious, legal, or economic choice, or a business decision. The purpose is usually to persuade others to accept your unproven idea.

Example: We should delay reorganizing our department.

Your presentation should:

- State your opinion.
- Establish significance.
- Give reasons.
- Project implications and outcomes.
- Summarize and draw conclusions.

Thesis Pattern

Unlike an opinion, a thesis can be tested, either by logic, evidence, or experiment. Ultimately, it can be proved right or wrong.

Example: Updating our computer system, rather than hiring additional personnel, will prove cost-effective within two years.

Your presentation should:

- State the thesis.
- Show implications.
- List proofs.
- Summarize and draw conclusions.

Instruction Pattern

Instruction presentations teach a way to do something.

Example: How to write more effective memos.

Your presentation should:

- State the purpose.
- List steps.
- Summarize.

Information Pattern

Informational presentations provide facts and explanations of facts. Typically, the goal is to present data, not to draw conclusions, to persuade, or to prove.

Example: An interim report on current research.

Your presentation should:

- Announce subject and purpose.
- Tell who, what, where, when, how, and why.
- Summarize.
- Lay out facts, explain implications.
- Summarize.

Primary and Secondary Purposes

All five patterns obviously have a good deal in common. For that reason, there are bound to be overlaps. The crucial task is to decide which purpose is primary and use that one to organize your structure. The other purposes can then play secondary and supportive roles. Once that is done, everything will fall into place.

Two brief exercises will help get your intentions clear.

Clarity Exercise #1

As you proceed in your research, keep checking your intention.

State your topic. Reduce it to one sentence suitable to be used as an

opening: _____

_____

_____

_____

Summarize your conclusion. Reduce it to one sentence suitable to be

used as a closing: _____

_____

_____

_____

Does this topic and conclusion most nearly relate to:
  Solving a problem? _____
  Arguing an opinion? _____
  Proving a thesis? _____
  Communicating information? _____
  Giving instructions? _____

Repeat this process on a regular basis. Keep in mind that what you think will be a *thesis* may turn out to be only an *opinion*. Or that the marshaling of your *information* may turn up an unexpected and significant *problem*. In this case, ask yourself:

Clarity Exercise #2

If I am veering away from my original intention, would it be better to:

Revert back? ____

Follow my new direction? ____

Why so? _____

_____

_____

_____

_____

Clarification Plus

Aside from clarifying your focus, there are two added benefits to practicing these exercises.

First, you will learn to recognize these patterns in other people's work. This awareness will increase your efficiency in extracting information.

Second, without even trying, you will automatically compose and memorize your opening and closing sentences. This will give you an enormous head start in getting your presentation ready.

A Generic Pattern

All five structural patterns follow a common rhythm, one that seems to come from some very deep level in the human psyche. Being aware of this underlying pattern will give you such powerful insights that you will wonder how you ever got along without it.

This generic rhythm or pattern is not found only in presentations, but also in novels, plays, and movies, and in music. What all these have in common is that we perceive them sequentially, we follow them in time. To do this we need maps, landmarks, directional signals, and guideposts. That's where the pattern comes in.

Many plays, movies and novels follow a basic plot line:

Characters and situation established
First complication
Second and later complications
Climax
Resolution

Many musical pieces follow a similar form:

Key, tempo, and mood established
First theme and variations
Second and later themes and variations
Climax
Resolution

The common structure that underlies the five Patterns of Organization is strikingly similar:

Announcement of subject and purpose
First example
Second and later examples
Summary
Conclusion

The accompanying chart shows the common structural features of all good presentations.

1. The Problem Pattern:
To move to action
    State the problem
    Demonstrate the effects
    Trace the causes
    Offer solutions
    Summarize

2. The Opinion Pattern:
To persuade
    State your opinion
    Establish significance
    Give reasons
    Project implications
    Summarize and draw conclusions

3. The Thesis Pattern:
To prove something
    State the thesis
    Show implications
    List proofs
    Summarize and draw conclusions

4. The Instruction Pattern:
To instruct
    Materials (optional)
    State the purpose
    List steps
    Summarize

5. The Informational Pattern:
To share information
Tell who
  —what
  —where
  —when
  —how
  —why
Summarize

Using Key Phrases as Themes

Another powerful organizational tool is the use of key phrases. Themes can be announced, repeated, then brought back in different contexts, much like motifs in music.

In giving a speech called "The Corporation of the Future," for example, you might use that key phrase each time you introduce a new feature or aspect. By this simple means, you will help your listeners associate the various aspects of the subject with the subject itself:

> *The most visible difference between **the corporation of the future** and the corporation of the present will be . . .*
>
> *That is why I described **the corporation of the future** as a corporation without boundaries . . .*
>
> *Of the many changes shaping **the corporation of the future,** four stand out . . .*
>
> *And this brings me to time compression, which is the third factor shaping **the corporation of the future** . . .*

This kind of repetition, which always mixes new material with the old, is one of the most powerful structuring devices available to you. Each time you use it, you guide your listeners to a clearer and more comprehensive understanding of the topic as a whole.

Four or five such phrases can be used in any presentation of a half hour or more. They should contain in embryo all the major points you want to make. Getting them clear in your own mind will help immeasurably in composing and remembering your speech. Heard by your audience, they will constitute landmarks and direction signals that will tell them where they are, where they've been, and where they're going.

COMPOSITION

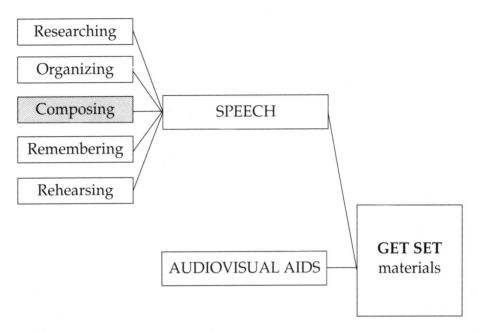

The lines between organizing and composing are as hard to draw as those between researching and organizing or remembering and rehearsing. This is so because all are stages in a single process.

Storyboarding

Now comes the time to use all those index cards you have been accumulating throughout your research. In the movie and TV industries, writers and directors make what they call "storyboards" to keep track of continuity. Whole walls are used as corkboards, on which sketches or file cards summarizing scenes are pinned up in rows, so those in charge can check that every scene is accounted for and in the right place.

Storyboarding is just as useful when it comes to organizing presentations. Find yourself a big open space, such as your living room floor, a study wall, or a large corkboard. Lay out your index cards, according to the order in which you think you will use them, from the Introduction through the Body to the Conclusion. Put a couple of key words on top, to identify the subtopic. Now, see what you've got.

Is there a better order? Experiment.

What is missing? A transition? Write one on a fresh card. A necessary bit of data? Make a note to look it up. Fill in as many blanks as you can for now, and use your next research period to find what you need to fill in the rest. Repeat the process until your structure is complete, your main ideas and images are in place, and your data is in your hands. In other words, until you have a digest of your entire presentation in visible form.

Storyboard for "The Corporation Without Boundaries"

(1) OPENING	(2) INTRO	(3) INTRO	(4) INTRO
"I'm going to talk about the corporation of the future, an ambitious and somewhat risky subject in these days of accelerating change."	Century ago: major worry about future, streets clogged with horse manure. (Have some fun.)	"Most visible difference will be in the makeup of the work force and the roles, etc., of its people."	German writer Goethe: "We see only what we look for, and we look for only what we know." To thrive in the time of change, must overcome old ideas and outdated notions.
(5) INTRO—MAIN POINT Managing corporate change	**(6) INTRO—DEFINITION & FOCUS** Corporation of the Future = CORPORATION WITHOUT BOUNDARIES A place where employees tap full potential: have responsibility, resources; make decisions, feel like owners = DRIVING FORCE OF FUTURE	**(7) BODY—STRUCTURE** FOUR MAJOR SOURCES OF CHANGE 1. Technology 2. Globalization 3. Telescoping of time 4. WORK FORCE ITSELF	**(8) TECHNOLOGY—ILLUSTRATION** Magnified opportunities—can't have a narrow vision. Thomas Edison—interested in *everything*.
(9) TECHNOLOGY Tech = powerful equalizer. Distributes access to info. Knowledge is power.	**(10) TECH/TRANSITION** Impact on structure: Supervisors must "relinquish some responsibility & empower subordinates." Supervisor/worker boundaries fading, like national boundaries.	**(11) GLOBALIZATION** "Brings me to 2nd major factor, Globalization." National boundaries going in TRADE, MANUFACTURING, CULTURE, ACCESS TO CAPITAL Euro-unity in 1992—L/S in Hungary	**(12) GLOBALIZATION** IMPACT ON WORK HOURS at L/S Expanding work day, shrinking time to get things done
(13) TRANS/TIME COMPRESSION "Brings me to third factor, Time Compression." Instant access has impact even on pants-making. Apparel a fad-driven industry.	**(14) TIME** "L/S recently cut in half the time it takes to turn a designer concept into an item on the sales floor." Competitive forces = speed up or fall behind.	**(15) TIME** "Quicker response and reply time" requires empowered employees. Employee empowerment = corporate success. Revolutionary War: British generals couldn't make on-spot decisions, so lost.	**(16) TRANS/WORK FORCE** "Importance of empowerment leads to last, most critical factor—work force."

(17) WORK FORCE By the year 2000— Only 15% entering workers white males. ⅔ female. Many immigrants of varying skills.	**(18) WORK FORCE** Department of Labor calls it THE SKILLS GAP— greater skills needed, less available. Business must educate work force. Education must continue through life.	**(19) WORK FORCE** "Business already spending $30 to $40 billion per year on job training. Must go way, way up."	**(20) WORK FORCE** C w/o B must accommodate rapid and dramatic *changes in family and social structures.* Need for more corporate responsibility. Must "rethink boundaries between employees' personal and professional lives."
(21) WORK FORCE Business can *benefit* from rethinking relationship with schools, child care, etc. E.g., line blurring between work and retirement. McDonald's now hiring seniors.	**(22) WORK FORCE** Skilled employees will have *options*. Corpora- tions must *earn* loyalty and support by more than wages and benefits.	**(23) WORK FORCE** "Must restructure line dividing workers and managers."	**(24) WORK FORCE** Workers must be: consulted, recognized, empowered. Have voice in: decisions, production goals, monitoring plant, efficiency, hiring, and firing.
(25) TRANS/ SUMMARY These changes are what will bring about C w/o B: Cross-fertilization across lines—national, cultural, social. *Reduce distinction between owners and employees.*	**(26) SUMMARY** Characteristics of C w/o B: International outlook Educational function Two-way communication with workers Increased stake for workers	**(27) SUMMARY— EXAMPLES** EMPOWERED ORGANIZATION = HIGHEST FORM OF CORP W/O BOUNDARIES Preview of future at L/S October 89 SF earthquake Philippine coup attempts	**(28) SUMMARY** "Pessimists envision an America that shortly will find itself a second-rate competitor in the global marketplace." QUALITIES NEEDED TO COMPETE: flexibility, innovation, unleashing the potential of people
(29) SUMMARY— COMPARISON Managerial habits need breaking. Like quitting smoking. I find it personally difficult. All working on it at L/S.	**(30) CONCLUSION** "It's my hope that businesses and other kinds of institutions will also strive to overcome their own boundaries, to unleash the potential of their people. If so, the result will be a more exciting, prosperous, and humane future for ourselves and for our children."		

Once your storyboard is finished, the composing phase is practically done. So is the memorization process. If you are going to use notes, they're all there on the cards.

Although the information for a storyboard can be stored in a computer, and most programs allow information to be moved around, computer screens are far too small for storyboarding. The whole point is to have your quotations, key phrases, topic sentences, transitions, and conclusions all visibly in front of you in one place at one time—to scan, check on, analyze, and shift around. Fitting each part into its place, like pieces into a jigsaw, requires you to be able to see the pattern as a whole.

Let's imagine that an executive at Levi Strauss is working on that speech called "The Corporation Without Boundaries." Let's say he intends to use examples from the history of his own company. His storyboard might look something like this:

Composing/Remembering

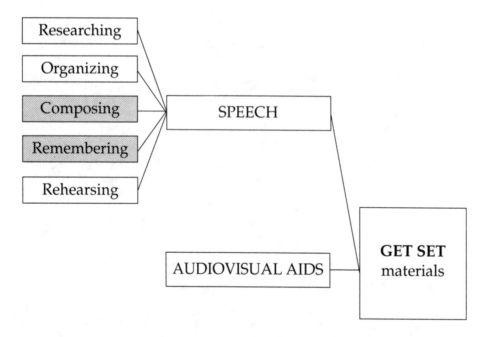

As you approach the completion of your storyboard, you will discover that your presentation has virtually composed itself. Don't worry. Be happy. Not everyone writes out presentations and not every presentation should be written out. Once the process of storyboarding has fixed your materials in your mind, that could be all you need. Some very practiced and accomplished speakers don't even need physical storyboards. They construct them mentally and carry them around in their heads.

When Is It Unnecessary to Write a Speech?

Virtually any time you'd rather not do it. Like millions of people, you may be inhibited by the act of writing. As soon as you "take pen in hand," you may start coming up with stilted phrases and artificial sequences of ideas. Or, like millions of others, you may be a virtual writing phobic, paralyzed by some diabolical inner force that compels you to stare for hours at blank sheets of paper or monitor screens. Why waste all that time?

Besides, if you write your speech you will be tempted to read it. And unless you are making some kind of announcement liable to be misconstrued in a courtroom or the media, reading your speech is about the least desirable of your alternatives.

Then Why Bother Writing at All?

Because it's such a superb memory device. Nothing else fixes a sequence of ideas more firmly in the mind than running it from your head through your hand. That's why old-fashioned teachers used to send naughty kids to the blackboard for a hundred rounds of "I will not whisper in class." And that's also why modern gurus instruct their followers to keep writing their daily affirmations until they get writer's cramp.

Writing combines kinesthetic memory (the movement of the fingers) with visual memory (the sight of the words) with aural memory (the sound of the words read back). It's a powerful package.

So what do I recommend? Write, but mainly as a memory aid. Expand your storyboard notes into simple, clear unpretentious prose. Don't take the process seriously. Remember that once you are up in front of the crowd, you will almost surely want to cut free from your written text.

What to Concentrate on in Your Writing

1. *Follow the structural principles established for your Basic Pattern of Organization.* Define in unambiguous terms your Subject, Purpose, and Focus. Be as clear as possible. Your intention is not to confront your audience with a mystery, but to communicate. Tell your listeners what you are going to do. Use key phrases to keep them oriented.

On card 7 of the storyboard, the writer lists four major "sources" of change. The rest of the speech consists of dealing with those four sources in order. Each time he makes a transition from one source to another, he announces the shift. This is what's known as giving the listener a *map*.

2. *Use transitions.* Points should not be made in random order. There should always be a logical or structural reason why point B follows point

A and point C follows point B. Every time you shift from one point to the next, make a clear directional statement to announce the change—in other words, refer your listeners to their map.

3. *Remember the limits of aural perception and memory.* Studies have shown that we remember far more of what we see than what we hear—of what we read than what is told to us. This is especially true of people nurtured on TV. Speeches, therefore, have to be almost simplistic. They have to spell things out and keep spelling them out, or listeners get lost. An elegant and complex prose style may be wonderfully impressive in an essay, but it has no place in modern speechmaking.

4. *Use examples, stories, humor, and images.* Anything that varies the monotony of facts and argumentation will relax your audience and focus attention. Stories, both serious and comic, will stick in a listener's mind far longer than any bare-bones assertion. All the great communicators have known this, from the days of Buddha and Socrates to Ronald Reagan. Jesus scarcely ever expressed an idea without illustrating it with a parable. Since visual memory is so much stronger than verbal memory, ideas that are turned into images are the ones that endure.

Dr. Janelle Barlow, who gives unforgettable speeches on time management, brings out a single brown paper supermarket bag, along with six typical grocery products. Tossing the products helter-skelter into the bag, she says, "Some people are single-baggers. They're in such a hurry they just throw the stuff in, giving the bag maybe a fifty-fifty chance of surviving the trip to your kitchen." Then she empties the single bag, reinforces it with a second one, and carefully fits the items inside, meanwhile saying, "And some people are double-baggers, carefully arranging the products so that you know you will get everything home intact." Then she simply asks, "Which kind of person are you?"

This clever bit of business demonstrates the power both of examples and images. No amount of lecturing on "Haste makes waste" could ever achieve an equal impact.

Use Basic Rhetorical Devices

Rhetoric, the technical term for the craft of speechmaking, was once a major subject in schools. Students learned both to recognize and to use a whole complex of rhetorical devices. Today, because of the lack of such training, I advise speakers to use as simple a style as possible, avoiding all but the most basic figures of speech.

The rhetorical devices still commonly used and understood are these:

1. **Comparison and contrast.** *The past vs. the present. Slides vs. overhead projectors. Life in China vs. life in Japan.* Likenesses and differences can be clarified by discussing them one aspect at a time. It's a technique to be used frequently and freely.

2. **Rhetorical questions.** *Why do I insist on discussing our negative cash flow? Because the future of our company depends on our immediate response.* Asking questions and then answering them can be very effective, but it rapidly becomes ineffective if overdone. Use no more than one or two rhetorical questions in any one speech, and only if and when the topic is urgent.

3. **The Rule of Three.** *The lame, the halt, and the blind. Of the people, by the people, for the people. Yes, no, and maybe. Wine, women, and song. I came, I saw, I conquered. Blood, sweat, and tears.* For some mysterious reason, ideas presented in threes are memorable. Use tricolons, but only occasionally, where you want to give emphasis.

In the past, other devices were commonly used, such as *anaphora* (beginning a series of sentences alike), *hyperbole* (exaggerating for effect), *alliteration* (using series of words beginning with the same letter), *ellipsis* and *asyndeton* (omitting words and using sentence fragments to make the pace more urgent), and *balance* (pairing sentences with the same structure). These tend to be much too formal and grandiose for modern taste. They are used these days mainly on very formal occasions such as inaugural addresses, or from the pulpit or soap box.

The Last Word on Structure

**Don't rely on your audience to follow you.
Lead them.**

Remembering/Rehearsing

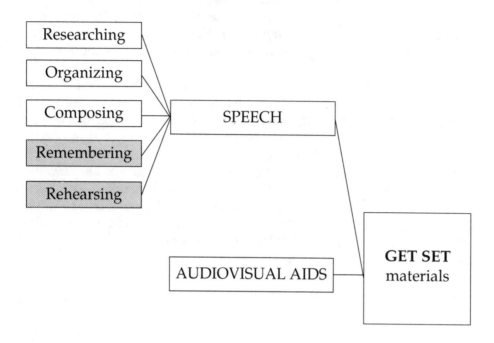

The Man of the Year

I am now going to take my own excellent advice and tell a true story.

Mark, a client of mine, had been named Man of the Year by a national civic organization. He had written a really fine acceptance speech and I was coaching him in its delivery. He had become fixed on the idea of memorizing it verbatim and reciting it back by rote.

I tried to dissuade him. "It's too dangerous, Mark. If you lose your place, you could lose your cool right along with it."

"Look, I want to give it exactly the way it's written," he kept insisting. "That's what I'm here for. Because you're a memory expert."

Since he was intransigent, I decided to try a little judo. "Okay," I agreed. "Let's do it your way. You recite from memory, and I'll get it on tape so you can hear it back."

I turned on the recorder and Mark turned on his speech. For a few minutes, all went well. Then he got lost and had to refer to his script. He was fluent for a while, then stopped to hunt for his place again. But on the whole he remembered well and was pleased with the result.

I congratulated him, then asked if he was willing to be frivolous for the next fifteen minutes, and just say his memorized first line and go freely from there. I said to imagine that he was a hang glider, taking a practiced leap from a high peak, then letting the wind carry him over the wide valleys. "Trust that your unconscious mind will work on all your knowledge and provide a good order," I suggested.

He agreed and tried it. When he was done, I played back the tape. First we heard Mark's memorized speech. Then we heard the improvised one.

Mark was astounded at the contrast. The improvised speech was so much more vital, so much more exciting, so much more compelling. True, some of his favorite phrases were missing, but what replaced them were just as good, in fact better. The next morning, in the ballroom of a world-renowned hotel, Mark took the leap. He opened and closed with his memorized lines and relied on his preparation, his knowledge, his imagination and enthusiasm to get him through the rest.

Actually, it was not quite that simple. In between, I had spent a couple of minutes teaching Mark an easy mnemonic technique for remembering ten ideas, a technique I'll be teaching you in just a moment. This additional strategy gave him the confidence of knowing he would not leave out anything of significance.

Fear of Forgetting

One of the main causes of speaker anxiety is the fear of forgetting. Few people would mind getting up to speak if their heads were equipped with internal cassette players that spoke their speeches for them, or if they could play dummy to some invisible ventriloquist.

Naturally, speakers who are that anxious imagine that memorization will help. They will turn themselves into human tape recorders and reel away. Or better yet, they'll simply read their speeches word for word. Unfortunately, these supposed solutions rarely work.

Why Memorization Is a Trap

Getting an entire speech by heart is an extremely arduous and time-consuming process. Worse than that, it is *dangerous*. One lapse of memory can leave you with your jaw hanging open, literally speechless. And if you're nervous about speaking in the first place, what happens to you then?

When you speak by rote, you concentrate on the words, not on what you're saying. This leads to goofs, sometimes embarrassing ones. In the thirties and forties, there was a popular MGM actor named Walter Pidgeon, whose specialty was playing very dignified characters. At the end of a live radio interview the interviewer rushed to close with the usual canned and automatic remarks. "Mr. Pleasure," he gushed. "This has been a Pidgeon." Fifty years later, this goof is still remembered by media professionals.

Speaking from a can always carries the threat of such disasters.

True, there are times when memorization is required. Sales reps who are given scripts, for example, are instructed to deliver them verbatim.

But sales scripts are short and usually supported by visual aids that serve as mnemonic devices. For all that, once out in the field, good reps usually ignore instructions and freely adjust their scripts to the responses of individual prospects.

Why Reading Only Makes Matters Worse

Keeping audience attention is dependent on maintaining eye contact and personal interchange. Few speakers can do that when their gaze is fixed on a written text. Conditioned by sad experience, audiences turn off at the mere sight of a speaker with a sheaf of papers. They expect to be put to sleep, and usually are.

There are, of course, exceptions. Politicians who send written texts to the press need to make sure what comes out of their mouths will match. Nowadays, most people in office spend serious amounts of time and money being trained in acting skills. They are heavily rehearsed and work from scripts encoded with instructions governing every phrase. They learn to give performances that virtually disguise the fact that they are reading.

Like politicians, top executives also use excellent professional speech-writers and have little time for memorization. So they also tend to read. But unless they regularly work with acting coaches, or have great natural charisma and dramatic talent, their speeches turn out to be more interesting on paper than they are to hear.

Anything that *sounds* either read or memorized immediately loses credibility. It also loses that sense of *discovery* that the best speeches give— *the sensation of catching an exciting mind in the act of thinking.* This is the reason sales reps deliberately abandon the scripts they know by heart. They want their voices to express the sense of spontaneous discovery that they hope their prospects will feel.

The moral of this story is this: Even if you have written out a perfect speech—even if you've never created anything so glorious before, even if you can't help but imagine yourself delivering it word for word and entrancing the audience with your deathless prose, even if, like a new parent, you are blindly in love with your wondrous offspring—*do not be seduced into reciting it by rote or reading it—unless you have absolutely no other choice.*

What to Do Instead

Personally, I memorize only two brief passages, my first and my last. And I strongly advise clients to do the same.

Memorizing the first sentence creates a smooth opening. It gives you confidence. It warms you up. It provides the chance to make eye contact with your audience and win them over. Audiences depend on first impressions to determine how closely they will listen, so starting strong is one of the two most important things you can do.

Memorizing the last sentence creates a strong conclusion. It lets you end powerfully and leave a clear impression behind. Once again, you can look your audience in the eye. The last impression is the one audiences carry away, which makes ending strong the second of the two most important things you can do.

As for the rest, the rule is simple. *Memorize what you are going to say— not the words you are going to use.* Do this by fixing your ideas—your structure, your main points, your transitions, your key phrases—clearly in your mind.

My adaptation of the *Lessac system,* devised by Professor Arthur Lessac of the State University of New York, will help you do exactly that.

Modified Lessac Memory System

1. Complete your storyboard.
2. Divide your storyboard into sections short enough for you to master easily, one at a time.
3. Get comfortable with the first section.
4. Get up in front of an imaginary audience and talk on that section, with the help of your cards.
5. Put down your cards, then talk on that section naturally, in your own words. Don't be afraid to ad lib or change some of what you planned to say. Look into the eyes of your imaginary audience and answer the questions that come up. If you discover important new points as a result, add them to your storyboard.
6. Take up your cards again and deliver that section again, looking at your cards only when you absolutely *must.*
7. Put down your cards, and deliver that section again. Notice that as you get more exciting, your imaginary audience gets more excited.
8. Repeat these steps with each section of the speech, until you are completely at ease with the material.
9. Repeat the entire speech without notes. If you get stuck or leave something out, go back and mark it on your cards.
10. Take your cards with you as insurance on the day of the speech, but expect that you won't have to use them.

The Power of Mental Rehearsal

The effectiveness of "mental rehearsal," the technique I have just described, is powerfully confirmed by a study noted in Charles Garfield's

Peak Performers. A number of people who had expressed interest in a public speaking class were divided into three groups.

Group 1 took a course that assigned reading and study about public speaking but required no speeches. They did not improve.

Group 2 did similar readings and also gave two talks a week. They improved noticeably.

Group 3 did the reading, watched videotapes of good speakers, gave one talk a week, and rehearsed mentally twice a week. Although they spoke formally only half as much as the people in group 2, they improved far more.

Garfield also tells the story of Liu Chi Kung, a world-class concert pianist imprisoned for seven years during the Cultural Revolution in China. Upon his release, he immediately resumed his concert career, astonishing critics with his undiminished musicianship. Asked how he had kept up his skills without practice, he replied, "I did practice, every day. I rehearsed every piece I had ever played, note by note, in my mind."

How to Remember Ten Ideas in Two Minutes

Remember our Man of the Year? Before delivering his acceptance speech, he took out a "memory insurance policy." He learned my *Method of Remembering Ten Things in Less than Two Minutes*, which is foolproof for anyone with a visual imagination.

This method consists of identifying a series of ideas with your own body parts. The more startlingly visual you can make the association, the more memorable it will be.

You begin with 1) the top of your head and systematically proceed south via 2) your forehead, 3) your nose, 4) your mouth, 5) your throat, 6) your chest, 7) your belly button, 8) your hips, 9) your knees, and 10) your feet. With each one, you envision the involvement of an idea or key word with that part. (See the accompanying illustration.)

The Peg System

1. **The top of your head**
   Picture the first item on top of your head.
2. **Your forehead**
   It's a billboard advertising the second object.
3. **Your nose**
   It's a vending machine spurting out dozens of the third thing.
4. **Your mouth**
   It's a tunnel with the fourth item driving in or pouring out. Or your teeth or tongue become the object.
5. **Your throat**
   Imagine your throat is Tiffany's window. The object it holds is very, very precious.
6. **Your chest**
   Here the object is stored in duplicate like a pair of lungs.
7. **Your belly button**
   The object is glued there or flashing there.
8. **Your hips**
   Imagine your money belt's wallet bulging with your eighth item.
9. **Your knees**
   Picture yourself kneeling on the ninth object. Is it pleasant? Comfortable? Awful?
10. **Your feet**
    You stand on the tenth object. What does it feel like? What are your feet doing to the object?

For example, you might want to open your speech with a discussion of the "magnified opportunites" afforded by the newest technology. If you were having trouble remembering, you could imagine the word *technology* imprinted atop your head and enlarged through a magnifying glass. If you wanted to discuss *globalization* next, you might imagine your forehead swollen out like a globe and imprinted with a map of the world. The more extreme and ludicrous the imagery, the easier it would be to remember—and the harder to forget.

If more than ten reminders were necessary, you would be trying to remember too much. No speech under an hour's length should make more than ten *major* points, and minor ones can always be left out or substituted. If your transitions are logical, each idea should remind you of the one to follow. Mnemonic devices are merely insurance. Your best memory device is a good structure for comprehension.

Comprehension organizes facts. If you grasp the overall significance of the Civil War, you're not likely to forget about *Gettysburg* or the *Emancipation Proclamation*.

In *Keep 'em Laughin'*, author Jeanne Robertson compares speaking to a group to rafting on a flowing river, with the speaker and audience both aboard. "As long as the speaker's thoughts are organized in logical order, the trip will be smooth. Failing to put thoughts in a logical arrangement can be compared to trying to take the raft upstream."

A Brief Summary of Memory and Rehearsal Techniques

Highlight, underline, and use marginal notes or flag notes. Deciding which passages to emphasize will force you to stay alert. Later, when you reread, you can save time by skipping from main point to main point.

Write down relevant ideas and information. The act of writing concentrates attention and fixes things in the mind.

Use index cards for your note-taking. Put the relevant facts or quotes on one side and source information on the back. Not only can you use the cards for *storyboards*, you will also know where to look if you have to go back to the source for more information, or if you need to give a reference. If worse comes to worst, you even bring them to the speech to keep on hand as a good luck charm or insurance policy.

Use mnemonic devices. These memory tricks can be rhymes, such as *Thirty days hath September*, or metaphors, such as *Iron Curtain*, or acronyms, such as *MADD* (Mothers Against Drunk Driving) or *CORE* (Congress of Racial Equality). Or visual tricks such as the Ten Things system. Or make up your own.

Translate ideas into images. The odd and unusual sticks in our minds, so use incongruous or startling pictures. If you are trying to remember two couples named Sam and Olivia, Alice and Paul, then picture them all showering together with SOAP. If Paul breaks up with Alice and finds Ursula, cook them all in a SOUP. Such memory games are fun and incredibly effective.

Use refreshers. The mind is constantly accumulating new impressions. Inevitably, previous ones fade out or get shoved aside. Fortunately, a couple of minutes spent going over highlights, marginal notes, or index cards will usually trigger the return of information stored over many hours of research and preparation.

Rehearsing

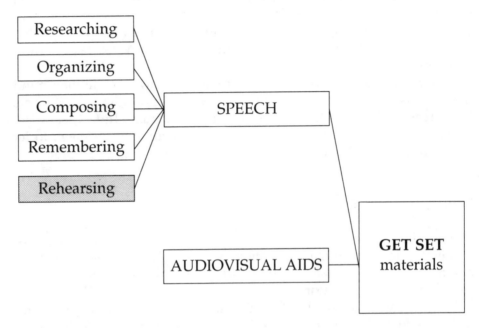

There's more to rehearsing than getting your ideas straight in your mind. You also must learn to make the best use of your voice and your presence.

Your Voice

When you are nervous about speaking or uncertain about what you have to say, you tend to raise your pitch and lower your volume. To speak successfully, you have to reverse the procedure.

Remember that intimate murmurs are lovely between loved ones in a quiet room. But public speaking requires projection.

Speak clearly. It's no use being heard if you're not understood. Remember that imperfect hearing is probably just as common as imperfect vision and far harder to correct.

Presentations require much clearer enunciation than conversations face to face. Don't mumble or drop your voice at the end of sentences. The custom of dropping the voice for emphasis, instead of raising it, recently became a fad. It sounds oh-so superior, cool, elegant, and understated (what the Japanese call *shibui*), but it creates a nightmare for audiences. They catch everything but what's most important. Have mercy and refrain.

Sound alive. Next to volume and clarity, vocal *delivery* is most important. *Vary* your speech. *Emphasize* important points. *Pause* between ideas. *Convey energy, excitement, conviction.* All this will come naturally if you are more interested in your subject than yourself, and if you are not reading from a script or reeling off something from memory.

When you rehearse, try to imitate a truly great actor or speaker giving your presentation. Since you're only rehearsing, and no one will hear you, feel free to be as dramatic and excited as you can be. Some of that excitement will stay with you, even when you give your speech in front of others.

Go faster, not slower. As every fluent reader knows, the human mind can process language far more quickly than the mouth can speak. This is the reason slow speakers drive their listeners crazy. In fact, slow delivery actually impedes comprehension by encouraging listeners to let their minds drift. Don't rush through your speech, but do be brisk.

Using the Tape Recorder

The best way to correct for volume and clarity (short of hiring expensive trainers) is to tape your presentations as you rehearse. Place your microphone several yards away, then, when you play back, notice which sounds come through clearly and which are faint or blurred. Correct until you come across distinctly at all times. This effort may frustrate and distract you at first, but will result in rapid and permanent improvement.

Your tape recorder is your best friend, but like all really good friends, it will sometimes tell you things you don't want to hear. Don't be distressed if your tone quality sounds alien and disconcerting. Your voice on tape doesn't sound much like your actual voice coming from your throat and vibrating through your body. But do be concerned if what you hear seems monotonous, expressionless, and flat.

Your Podium Presence

Since human beings pick up more information visually than any other way, your manner of standing and moving and gesturing are of great importance. And yet, hard-and-fast rules for podium behavior do not exist.

Ken W. Huskey, a noted public speaker and communications consultant, advises speakers not to put their hands on their hips, fold their arms on the podium, or grip the podium with their hands. Yet some of the most riveting speakers of modern times (such as President Kennedy) have done all of them. Some years back, speakers were advised not to use emphatic gestures. Today, most consultants say just the opposite.

In the past, speakers were taught to fold their hands modestly behind or in front of them. Such poses are now considered ridiculous.

The best general rule is to stand straight, be natural, and feel free to gesture as seems appropriate. Obviously, your demeanor should be friendly, pleasant, occasionally smiling yet serious, authoritative yet open to discussion and criticism, and relaxed. If you are all these, appropriate stance and gestures will follow naturally.

Using Videotape or Mirrors

A visual equivalent of taping your voice for sound is videotaping your body for gestures. Many communications specialists use video as a foremost tool. A majority of actors, dancers, athletes, and other performers have come to find it indispensable. If you have access to a camcorder, videotape a rehearsal or two. Nothing will teach you faster what needs correcting.

Before there were camcorders, there were mirrors. Actors, dancers, and speakers have rehearsed in front of them for centuries. If video equipment is unavailable, you can still make tremendous progress by giving your presentation to a mirror.

You may cringe at such a thought. All your faults on display! Won't it make you more self-conscious than ever? The answer is that it certainly will. All you will see at first will be faults. But unless you see them, you can't correct them.

You and Your Adrenaline

Understand that many of your faults are merely nervous mannerisms, ways of getting rid of the excess adrenaline surging through your system. Slicking back your hair, tapping your foot, touching your face, and clearing your throat are all mannerisms of this kind.

Many good speakers are aware of a precious secret. Biologically, it makes no difference at all whether you are excited, thrilled, in love, or scared to death. Your brain sends that same adrenaline rushing through your system.

Understanding this helped me overcome my own stage fright. I told myself that my heart was pounding from excitement, not fear. Instead of trying to get rid of my adrenaline rush through nervous mannerisms, I consciously directed it into energizing my performance.

You can do it too. The opportunity lies in your rehearsals in front of the mirror or camcorder. Even while you work to eliminate your nervous mannerisms, redirect your energy into the expression of real or pretended excitement. It's what actors do. It's what professional speakers do. It's what I do.

It works for us and it will also work for you.

The Perfect Presentation: Robert Haas's "The Corporation Without Boundaries"

Let's begin with a rhetorical question: Why show you this particular speech? Because it is truly contemporary. It does very well the sorts of things that business and professional people are called upon to do. It summarizes a present situation. It projects forward and tries to predict future trends. It does so in simple, clear, straightforward language. It employs facts skillfully, subordinating them to the main ideas. And it presents a model of clear, lucid structure.

It is not a speech for the ages. Nothing in it will endure as *"I have a dream," "Ich bin ein Berliner,"* or *"We have nothing to fear but fear itself."* And nothing in it should. After all, this is not a rallying cry by a political leader attempting to stir a mass audience. It is a presentation by a business professional to other business professionals, intended to put up ideas for consideration.

At first glance, you may suppose this is an *opinion* speech, an attempt to speculate on what the future will bring. Look again, and you will see that it is actually a *problem* speech: *The world is changing. How can we manage change? What solutions to our problems will make change work to our benefit instead of to our detriment?* Haas's tone is positive and enthusiastic. He wishes to treat the problem as an opportunity. But watch closely and note that this is his way of offering solutions, and that each new trend he raises for discussion is, in fact, a potential problem calling for a change in traditional managerial style.

Commentary

Storyboard and outline. Robert Haas's presentation will be accompanied by a storyboard and an outline. Now you will have a chance to see how they actually work.

You have seen the *storyboard* before, in the section on Composing. It is, of course, a fiction, a reconstruction of what *might* have gone into creating Haas's speech. Remember that each rectangle represents an index card, numbered and categorized according to its ultimate place in the presentation. A storyboard is a way to create a presentation. It assembles the pieces from which the final product will be made.

The *outline* (page 110) describes the final structure of the speech. Ideally, an outline should be written out *after* the presentation has been completed, to make sure that the structure is sound.

Marginal notes. We have run two kinds of marginal notes alongside the text of the speech.

First, you will find copies of the "index cards" from the storyboard alongside the passages they have generated. These will help you see how a speech is made from a storyboard.

We also point out particularly effective examples of storytelling, comparison and contrast, transitions, and the like. Most of these were covered earlier in the chapter, but we saved the subject of topic sentences until now, since we wanted the subject to be very fresh in your mind as you read this presentation.

Topic Sentences

A *topic sentence* defines the subject of a presentation, a section of a presentation, or a paragraph. It explicitly tells a reader or listener what you are going to discuss. It is at once a landmark and a directional signal. Without good topic sentences, and plenty of them, listeners will get lost. Haas employs topic sentences superbly.

At times, Haas's signals will seem a bit too frequent, a bit too obvious. This is so because you will be reading something that was meant to be heard. Remember, we humans learn less well through hearing than seeing. As a presenter, you have to cater to the ear. That means, you have to guide. You have to clarify. You have to repeat. You have to summarize. The trick is to add some fresh element each time around.

Weekly Program
Commonwealth Club
San Francisco
December 1, 1989

Robert Haas
Chairman of the Board and CEO
Levi Strauss and Company

Subject sentence

(1) OPENING

"I'm going to talk about the corporation of the future, an ambitious and somewhat risky subject in these days of accelerating change."

An opinion

(2) INTRO

Century ago: major worry about future, streets clogged with horse manure. (Have some fun.)

Humor—not a joke

Good afternoon. Thank you, Mr. Chow, for your generous remarks. This afternoon I'm going to talk about the corporation of the future, an ambitious and somewhat risky subject in these days of accelerating change. The risk comes because we all make predictions by working with current trends. And these can be quickly outdated.

For example, imagine if we asked people one hundred years ago to envision our cities today, using their transportation modes of the time and population trends. Chances are high they'd quicky identify at least one major problem—streets absolutely buried under horse manure. You have no idea how restrained I had to be in not playing around with that image. I can see we have a number of potential speechwriters in the audience, too.

I'm well aware that the change in the years to come may show the limitations of my own predictions. And yet, today I still intend to spend time telling you what I see in the future.

Why do I do this? Because I like the future I see. Because I think it offers hope and excitement for all of us. Because maybe if others share my vision about a future that can be, we'll move one step closer to making the future a reality.

All of us today are now embarked on a wondrous and somewhat scary journey to a world vastly transformed by the forces of change. Institutions as well as individuals will thrive or decline, depending on their ability to understand the implications of these forces. Now, I wish I could stand here and paint for you a detailed picture of the corporations in the year 2000, but, to be honest with you, I cannot. Change is simply too rapid. The impact of new technologies, the tremendous social and political transformations, here in the U.S. and abroad, the emergence of new economic relationships and financial practices: all of these make predictions perilous if not impossible.

I can, however, gaze into my crystal ball and reveal one certainty. Not only will the future be different, but all of us, especially managers and employees, will be different as well.

The most visible differences between the corporation of the future and the present day counterpart will be in the makeup of the work force, and the roles, relationships, and responsibilities of its people. Not the types of products they make, nor the equipment they use in factories (although these certainly will be very different), but who is working, how they will be working, why they will be working, and what work will mean to them.

Now, a good first step in dealing with change is to test all your assumptions. Every day old truisms fall by the wayside and traditional concepts are being challenged. New opportunities emerge, but do we see them clearly? The German writer Goethe touched on this when he said, "We see only what we look for, and we look for only what we know." Sometimes we think we know what we can and cannot do, but this is based on the world as it was, rather than the world as it is or could be.

Companies intent on surviving and thriving must help their employees overcome their old ideas and outdated notions, whether this means seeking opportunities in new markets, acting with greater urgency, treating suppliers

Engage audience

Purpose

Topic sentence of paragraph

Implications for management

Topic sentence

(3) INTRO

"Most visible difference will be in the makeup of the work force and the roles, etc., of its people."

Topic sentence

(4) INTRO

German writer Goethe: "We see only what we look for, and we look for only what we know."

To thrive in the time of change, must overcome old ideas and outdated notions.

Implication

(5) INTRO—MAIN POINT

Managing corporate change

**(6) INTRO—
    DEFINITION & FOCUS**

Corporation of the Future = CORPORA-
TION WITHOUT BOUNDARIES

A place where employees tap full potential: have responsibility, resources; make
decisions, feel like owners = DRIVING
FORCE OF FUTURE

Introduction of "empowerment"

(7) BODY—STRUCTURE

FOUR MAJOR SOURCES OF CHANGE
1 Technology
2 Globalization
3 Telescoping of time
4 WORK FORCE ITSELF

Topic sentence—technology

Examples

Implications for business

Examples

Relevance to speaker's experience

and customers as partners, rethinking the distinction between workers and managers, or redrawing the lines between personal and professional concerns.

Familiar boundaries are being breached, or are disap-
pearing altogether. This is why I described the corporation
of the future as the corporation without boundaries. In a
corporation without boundaries, employees are able to tap
their fullest potential. They know what they're responsible
for, and what resources they have to get the job done.
They're empowered to make their own decisions. They
take personal responsibility for their contribution to the
business. They feel like owners, and, in many cases, they
will be.

Empowered employees are the driving force of the corporation of the future. But, in a way, I'm getting ahead of
my story. There's more that needs to be said about change
and why it will require companies and managers to shift
greater responsibility, and authority, to employees.

Of the many changes shaping the corporation of the
future, four stand out in my view. First, the impact of
technology. Second, the globalization of enterprises.
Third, the telescoping of time. And, finally, changes in
the work force itself. Let me start with a few words about
technology.

Technology is the most potent force we have to quickly
erase old boundaries and assumptions. Its change is the
most pervasive and tangible. Examples of new technology
affecting our daily activities are almost limitless. Computers that make possible everything from automatic teller
machines to talking cars. Satellites that warn of approach-
ing hurricanes or link offices around the globe. New phar-
maceuticals that mimic the body's natural defenses.

In the business world, technology is the most obvious
means of gaining a competitive advantage. To a small business, this may take the form of a new payroll accounting
system. To large corporations, the development of their
own robots. Nations, too, see technology as a means of
competition. Japan, for example, has already committed
significant resources to gain an edge in superconductors.

Now, some of you may be wondering if technology is
really that relevant for somebody whose company cuts and
sews pants. After all, Levi Strauss and Company is best
known for a product invented nearly 140 years ago, and
in some ways, that product hasn't changed very much.

Now, I'll bet that if my great-great-grand-uncle Levi
Strauss showed up today, he'd have little trouble seeing

our popular 501 jeans as the logical descendant of his original waist-high overalls. However, I know he'd be astonished at the way this enduring product is being manufactured, distributed, and marketed.

To put it simply, at Levi Strauss and Company technology is improving every aspect of our business. Computers help us identify trends, plan work flow, control our broad-based businesses. In our most advanced facility, transporters move the materials from station to station, and robots link our transporters to automated sewing equipment.

More examples from Levi Strauss

Instead of making decisions based on what consumers bought in the past, we're using computers to design and market test products before we buy the first bolt of cloth. This way, we can tell what the hot items will be six months before they arrive in stores. Now, you've heard of supply-side economics—we're engaged in demand-side manufacturing.

Another implication

Technological change magnifies future opportunities and uncertainties, so competitive corporations are mastering a whole new set of technologies. For example, no longer can our company focus only on machines that stitch fabric. Today, we've got to keep abreast of chemical processes, satellite communications, ergonomics, environmental issues, and a whole host of other developments. We should probably be keeping a close eye on microbiology and genetic engineering as well, because changes in these areas could radically affect cotton, our principal raw material. In five years, they probably will.

> **(8) TECHNOLOGY—ILLUSTRATION**
> Magnified opportunities—can't have a narrow vision.
>
> Thomas Edison—interested in *everything*.

I'm reminded of a story about Thomas Edison who was once asked to sign a guest book. Now, it had the usual columns for name and address, and then there was one that asked what the individual was interested in. Edison had a simple, one-word reply: everything. The man who invented the electric light bulb, motion pictures, and the gramophone, knew that to harness the forces of technology, you cannot have a narrow vision. You must be open to everything.

Illustration

Technology, especially in the area of computers, is a powerful equalizer. Access to information, once held captive in big mainframes, and only to wizards with the right codes, is being distributed more broadly. So, if knowledge is power, that power today is being shared in many ways, with extraordinary ramifications for the business world. Information can now be transmitted globally in a matter

Topic sentence

> **(9) TECHNOLOGY**
> Tech = powerful equalizer. Distributes access to info. Knowledge is power.

of seconds. It is no longer constrained by the cumbersome limitations of organizational chain of command, paperwork, or the mails. Offices in employee homes far from corporate headquarters can tap into a vast network of data.

People at every level of the corporation are gaining the ability to work smarter and more independently. As we fully harness the computer's potential, the capabilites of all our employees—pattern cutters and lawyers, plant managers and secretaries—will broaden and improve greatly. This transformation must be overseen by supervisors who are willing to relinquish some of their responsibilities, and empower their subordinates.

While technology allows corporations to make startling advances, it also opens them to challenges from many new directions. Long-standing competitive advantages may disappear overnight. Past experience in proprietary products, or manufacturing processes, boundaries that once provided a competitive advantage, can now quickly fade in importance. Also fading are geographic distinctions that historically have placed barriers to foreign competition.

This brings me to the second major change factor—globalization. In times past, geography determined plant locations and production distribution. More recently, a country's borders defined individual markets. These were shaped by individual laws, customs, currencies, and language.

Today we already know that national boundaries are becoming less of an obstacle. The recent U.S./Canada trade agreement is one example. Western Europe's striving for economic unity in 1992, and the breaking down of barriers in Eastern Europe are events of even greater significance. Many companies are now developing businesses in Eastern European and Soviet markets. In Hungary, for example, Levi Strauss and Company has made a profit and found new customers. In turn, Hungarians have gained new technologies, raised product quality standards, and earned better wages than ever before.

We're witnessing the globalization of the manufacturing process as well. This represents a triumph over old geographic limitations. Our company, for example, buys denim from a mill in North Carolina, ships it to France where it is sewed into jeans, launders these jeans in Belgium, and markets them in West Germany, using television commercials that were produced in England.

We are a global company by many traditional standards.

Implication for managers

---

(10) TECH/TRANSITION

Impact on structure:
Supervisors must "relinquish some responsibility & empower subordinates."
Supervisor/worker boundaries fading, like national boundaries.

Examples

---

(11) GLOBALIZATION

"Brings me to 2nd major factor, Globalization."
National boundaries going in TRADE, MANUFACTURING, CULTURE, ACCESS TO CAPITAL
Euro-unity in 1992—L/S in Hungary

Past contrasted with present—examples

Trade

Manufacturing

Examples

We have employees in facilities in dozens of countries, we market internationally, and we look for new leadership talent around the globe.

But, remaining a truly global corporation requires tapping new resources. Key among these is the diversity of cultures and perspectives held by employees around the world. This diversity can be harnessed to make businesses more successful in international markets.

From a business perspective, one of the most important new resources available because of globalization and supported by technology is access to new capital. The ability to move funds electronically has literally transformed capital markets into a twenty-four-hour world marketplace. Now, when you accept the reality that businesses in time zones throughout the world are now linked, the implications are staggering.

New resources
Capital

Consider, for example, the now-outdated notion of regular work hours. Shouldn't a truly global corporation be open for business twenty-four hours a day? Somewhere in the world there are customers awake and ready to do business, co-workers eager for consultation, financiers ready to discuss new ventures. Should all this be put on hold just because it's after five P.M. in San Francisco? I think not. Technology is not only shrinking the globe and expanding the work day, it is also nurturing our impulse to get things done faster.

Implication—work hours

> **(12) GLOBALIZATION**
> IMPACT ON WORK HOURS at L/S
> Expanding work day, shrinking time to get things done

And this brings me to time compression, which is the third factor shaping the corporation of the future. Today, largely because of television, we have a different set of time expectations. Real-life dramas, like the protests in Tiananmen Square and in Prague, are instantly available to everyone. And in the world of make-believe television programs, even the thorniest conflicts seem to be resolved in minutes. The consequence of all this is that we increasingly live in a time-obsessed society. Photos are developed in an hour, eyeglass lenses are ground while you wait, fast food isn't just a Big Mac anymore, it's gourmet cooking to go, or Domino's pizza at your doorstep in thirty minutes.

> **(13) TRANS/TIME COMPRESSION**
> "Brings me to third factor, Time Compression." Instant access has impact even on pants-making.
> Apparel a fad-driven industry.

Examples

Today the ability to compress time can yield a competitive advantage. Conversely, the failure to deliver products and services to impatient customers can spell doom for any enterprise.

The fad-driven apparel industry is a perfect example. The look sported by Madonna in a rock video, or the sunglasses worn by Tom Cruise in a hit movie, can spur a

Application to Levi Strauss—own experience

Consequence and action taken

> **(14) TIME**
>
> "L/S recently cut in half the time it takes to turn a designer concept into an item on the sales floor." Competitive forces = speed up or fall behind.

More implications

> **(15) TIME**
>
> "Quicker response and reply time" requires empowered employees. Employee empowerment = corporate success. Revolutionary War: British generals couldn't make on-spot decisions, so lost.

Empowerment theme

Illustration:
opportunity lost because
empowerment lacking

Transition sentence

> **(16) TRANS/WORK FORCE**
>
> "Importance of empowerment leads to last, most critical factor—work force."

> **(17) WORK FORCE**
>
> By the year 2000—
> Only 15% entering workers white males.
> ⅔ female.
> Many immigrants of varying skills.

Statistics—few but telling

new style craze overnight. Eager consumers want that product, and they want it now. So, shortening the time to get a product to market is an ongoing necessity.

Responding to our customers' growing sense of urgency, Levi Strauss and Company has recently cut in half the time it takes to turn a designer concept into an item on the sales floor. Now, that may sound impressive, but to be honest, it's simply not good enough. There's a lot more time to be trimmed from the process, and we're already hard at work at that task.

Speed is essential not only in delivering your product to a breathless market, but in other business dealings as well. Telephones, fax machines, and electronic mail link the world. Business partners know that theoretically you can have near-instant access to information. So, not surprisingly, they expect you to be able to respond quickly with decisions. If you don't, somebody else in the marketplace will.

However, technology alone cannot make your company sufficiently responsive. To interact with business partners in a timely manner, global corporations must rely on well-informed employees who can be trusted to make decisions, and who accept the responsibility for results.

Here again, we find that empowerment is essential to success. Now, the value of empowerment is nothing new. History is filled with examples of opportunities lost because someone's on-the-spot representative would not, or could not, make the decision. One reason the British lost the Revolutionary War is because their generals had to wait for instructions from King George. Time was not on their side. The Colonists won.

The importance of empowerment leads me to the last, and in my view, the most critical area of change, the work force itself: its makeup, expectations, and needs. Remember, I said earlier that the only thing we know for sure is that in the future we will be different. Well, in that regard, the future is already here. Let's take a look at the United States between now and the year 2000.

First, there will be a significant decline in the percentage of white males, traditionally America's workers and managers. At the turn of the century, these men will account for only 15 percent of the people entering the work force. Women, on the other hand, will represent two thirds of the new entrants.

We can also expect an increasing proportion of minorities among the new employees. Some of these people will be skilled entrepreneurs or technicians with a track record of success. Others will be new to the world of business. Some will be immigrants, and some will not be comfortable with English.

The United States Department of Labor has identified what they've called a skills gap. This points to the disparity between the skills new jobs will require and the education and background new entrants bring to the workplace.

Many young people are not staying in school and even those who do may not be acquiring the skills they need: reading, writing, critical thinking, problem solving, science, and mathematics. At a time when the global marketplace makes it increasingly important to understand geography and to learn a second, and perhaps a third, language, we're graduating students who cannot locate Boston, let alone Brussels, on a map.

Now, I don't want to belabor what you've read and heard about in other places, but there's no escaping one critical fact: many new entrants to the work force are not well equipped to learn and to succeed at the kinds of jobs that need to get done.

To tackle this problem, we need to discard the old thinking that says, "Now you're a student. Now you're a worker." The concept of lifelong learning, the willingness and the ability to master new materials must replace the notion that education takes place only in schools. For the first time in our history, the majority of all new jobs will require a postsecondary education. Clearly, the skills gap is widening. Who's going to close that gap?

Well, let me give you a hint. The Department of Labor reports that private business is already spending $30 to $40 billion a year for formal on-the-job training. You can expect that number to go up, way up.

In coming years, we'll see even more two-wage-earner families, and more single-parent heads of households. This change from the traditional family, with the man as the only wage earner, is influencing how people feel about work, about the need for more flexible hours, their willingness to relocate, their desire to do some of their work at home. Employers will have to rethink the boundaries between employees' personal and professional lives. As these distinctions blur, corporations will also have to reexamine their involvement in functions formally performed by the family, neighborhood, or government.

Corporations without boundaries will rethink their re-

(18) **WORK FORCE**

Department of Labor calls it THE SKILLS GAP—greater skills needed, less available. Business must educate work force. Education must continue through life.

Examples of skills gap

Problem—causes

Question and answer

(19) **WORK FORCE**

"Business already spending $30 to $40 billion per year on job training. Must go way, way up."

Solution

(20) **WORK FORCE**

C w/o B must accommodate rapid and dramatic *changes in family and social structures*. Need for more corporate responsibility. Must "rethink boundaries between employees' personal and professional lives."

Role of business

> **(21) WORK FORCE**
>
> Business can *benefit* from rethinking relationship with schools, child care, etc.
>
> E.g., line blurring between work and retirement. McDonald's now hiring seniors.

Examples

Past, present, future

> **(22) WORK FORCE**
>
> Skilled employees will have *options*. Corporations must *earn* loyalty and support by more than wages and benefits.

lationship with institutions such as schools, seriously explore ways to address concerns such as child care, and consider stepping up to community involvement to tackle other concerns such as drugs, AIDS, and race relations.

Demographers tell us that in the future we can also expect more older workers to stay in the work force. They remain in their jobs for economic reasons, or perhaps, they'll stay on for social ones. But, whatever their motivation, we'll only be able to capitalize on their lifetime of skills and experiences if we discard the artificial boundary between being actively employed and retired. Between work supposedly appropriate for younger workers, but not for older ones.

Some businesses are already making headway in this regard. For example, when you go to a McDonald's restaurant nowadays, you may find a senior citizen taking your order, working effectively in a job previously held by a teenager.

In the future employees will challenge old distinctions, and seek greater flexibility on how and when they work. This seems only fair since companies have already begun discarding the traditional ground rules of employment.

In the good old days, employees offered their loyalty in exchange for job security, decent wages, and fair working conditions. Upheavals in the business world in recent years, however, have raised uncertainties in the relationship between employer and employee. Corporations in the future will have to earn the loyalty and support of their workers in many new ways. This will require among other changes new ways of managing.

Now, companies have always understood that customers are volunteers. They can choose our products and services or they can choose someone else's. Today we need to see that employees as well are really volunteers. They have options. If we're going to persuade the best people to choose us, and to stay with us, we must develop a new kind of work ethic.

But the time and resources that this will require is something new for many of us. We will still have to provide competitive wages and benefits, but we need to do much more. Employees want to be consulted and understand the thinking behind decisions. They want communication, not direction. They want recognition, and they want to be empowered to make decisions without having them ratified with layers of management.

As a first step in meeting these needs, companies will have to restructure. They must streamline to speed decisions. They must also provide more information, authority, and responsibility to those who are closest to products and consumers. Many companies, including our own, have already started this process.

(23) WORK FORCE

"Must restructure line dividing workers and managers."

Also, corporations will have to commit themselves to reworking one of the most rigid boundaries of all—the line that distinguishes workers and managers.

This means some basic assumptions need to be challenged. Why can't employees set production goals? Why can't they monitor plant efficiency? Why can't they hire and fire new employees, upon whom they're increasingly dependent? And why can't they benefit directly from their initiatives, which result in higher profits? Asking, and responding to, such questions will bring about the corporation without boundaries.

Return to issue of empowering workers in corporations without boundaries

Examples

(24) WORK FORCE

Workers must be: consulted, recognized, empowered. Have voice in: decisions, production goals, monitoring plant, efficiency, hiring and firing.

The corporation without boundaries must also have a truly international outlook. To do that, it will value and promote far more diversity than is common today. It will be committed to a cross-fertilization of ideas and values among its domestic and international work forces.

Cultural diversity

(25) TRANS/SUMMARY

These changes are what will bring about C w/o B: Cross-fertilization across lines—national, cultural, social.

Reduce distinction between owners and employees.

The corporation without boundaries will constantly seek ways to inform and educate people so they can challenge their own assumptions, their own ingrained ways of thinking. Also, its managers will do as much listening as talking.

A commitment to two-way communication will result in a work force that shares a common vision, a sense of direction, an understanding of values, ethics and standards. Without this individual decision making is crippled.

(26) SUMMARY

Characteristics of C w/o B:

International outlook
Educational function
Two-way communication with workers
Increased stake for workers

To promote initiative, creativity, and commitment, in the corporation without boundaries, managers must shed traditional authoritarian practices. Instead, they must be coaches, facilitators, and role models. By example they'll show that everyone within the corporation must look to one another as a resource, regardless of title, job description, or formal training.

The corporation without boundaries will also reduce the distinction between workers and owners. Its employees will gain an increasing stake in the success of the company, and a proportionate say in the discussions of company policies.

(27) SUMMARY—EXAMPLES

EMPOWERED ORGANIZATION = HIGHEST FORM OF CORP W/O BOUNDARIES

Preview of future at L/S
October 89 SF earthquake
Philippine coup attempts

What I've been describing is the empowered organization, the most advanced form of the corporation without boundaries that I can currently envision. At Levi Strauss and Company we have been promoting the concept of empowerment in recent years. Now, in many ways this looks like a return to the can-do spirit we enjoyed as a smaller company years ago. But the change we're striving for goes beyond feelings and attitudes. It's much more comprehensive.

Sometimes empowerment takes hold and sometimes it doesn't. It isn't just a tough change for managers; it's tough for employees as well. Oftentimes, both managers and employees are reluctant to let go of their traditional roles and power.

Personal examples

Frankly, it's a personal struggle for me as well. There's a lot of my own behavior I've been working to change. Happily, my colleagues don't hesitate to point out the areas in which improvement may be needed, or where progress has been made.

Humor

Recently, I had a most unexpected, but satisfying glimpse of how effective an empowered organization can be. I got a preview of the future in the aftermath of the October earthquake.

Earthquake

Fortunately, none of our employees was seriously injured. Our headquarters and other facilities suffered no significant damage. However, phones, computer systems, and normal electric service were out for some time.

Our headquarters was shut down for two days. For a company that does business in more than sixty countries, this raised serious questions about our ability to keep our global business up and running.

On the night of the quake, and over the next two days, we weren't able to contact all our headquarters staff. Most of you in the audience remember how difficult it was to telephone people living in the Bay Area at this time. Our managers and employees were put in a position where they had to make independent decisions about coming to work or staying home.

Well, do you know what happened? People made exactly the right decisions. The handful who did come in, many at great personal inconvenience, were just the ones who were essential at that time. The building operations staff, computer systems experts, production and customer service personnel, and others. Most people in these work units, and others in different departments, also made the correct decision. They stayed home. They planned their commute, and arranged child care while waiting to consult with their supervisors.

I hope we're not tested like that again, but I'm proud of the fact that when the test came, our people rose to the occasion. They exercised the initiative and showed the kind of commitment you'd expect from empowered employees.

Just this morning I got another example of how an empowered organization behaves. This was in association with the recent coup attempt in the Philippines.

Philippines

This morning in the Philippines, despite the disruption in Manila, 85 percent of our employees showed up for work. And, while we closed the factory and sent them home so that they would be safe and could be with their families, again it shows the kind of dedication that exists for the empowered organization.

Improvised—this happened today!

Our people in San Francisco and the Philippines demonstrated a true sense of psychic ownership, the pride employees feel when committed to their work. This pride is observable when you see people willing to make sacrifices, to take risks, to go beyond what's called for in a job description. These are the people who can successfully carry schools, government, non-profits, as well as corporations, into the future.

Psychic ownership

Pessimists envision an America that shortly will find itself a second-rate competitor in the global marketplace. I disagree.

Change is creating new markets and radically remaking existing ones. The key is flexibility, innovation, and a work force that can seize the moment. In the U.S. we have diversity within our borders, creative ferment in a culture that values initiative. If corporations empower their employees to tap these qualities, we'll surely remain a major commercial presence on the world stage. But we cannot underestimate the magnitude of this challenge.

> **(28) SUMMARY**
>
> "Pessimists envision an America that shortly will find itself a second-rate competitor in the global marketplace."
>
> QUALITIES NEEDED TO COMPETE: flexibility, innovation, unleashing the potential of people

Managing change is not a simple matter. In fact, nothing is more difficult. Implementing change within ourselves is difficult enough. Are there any former smokers in the audience? Implementing change among groups of people, or throughout institutions is exponentially more difficult.

Theme: managing change

> **(29) SUMMARY—COMPARISON**
>
> Managerial habits need breaking. Like quitting smoking.
>
> I find it personally difficult. All working on it at L/S.

Still, as the world continues its radical transformation, corporations intent on success will have to draw fully on every resource available. Mastering technology, having a global presence, and compressing response time will all prove invaluable, but the most important resource of all lies within people—their talent, energy, and commitment.

Summarize themes

A corporation without boundaries will best utilize all of these resources and that's the kind of corporation we're

(30) CONCLUSION

"It's my hope that businesses and other kinds of institutions will also strive to overcome their own boundaries, to unleash the potential of their people. If so, the result will be a more exciting, prosperous, and humane future for ourselves and for our children."

working to become at Levi Strauss and Company. It's my hope that businesses and other kinds of institutions will also strive to overcome their own boundaries, to unleash the potential of their people. And, if they do, the result will be a more exciting, prosperous, and humane future for ourselves and for our children.

Outline

INTRODUCTION: Corporation of the Future
  Subject: managing corporate change
  Purpose: listeners will understand and help shape it
  Central finding: changing function of the work force

BODY: Corporation of the Future = "Corporation Without Boundaries"

1. *Technology*

  Examples
  Magnified opportunities
    Examples
    Thomas Edison illustration
  Necessity for open vision
  Powerful equalizer—impacts on corporate structure

2. *Globalization*

  Contrast with past
  Impact on a) trade
           b) manufacturing process (Levi Strauss)
           c) cultural diversity
           d) sources of funding
           e) work hours and scheduling

3. *Time Compression*

  Examples
  Impact on Levi Strauss
  Impact on instant access
  Impact on personnel: examples

4. *Work Force* (most important—main topic)

  U.S. demographic changes: causes and effects
  "Skills gap": causes and effects
    Solution: more corporate continuing education
  Family structure: changes, causes and effects
    Solution: increasing corporate responsibility
  Older workers: blurring line between work and retirement
  Empowering workers: by breaking down barriers between workers and managers, workers and owners

CONCLUSION: "The Empowered Organization"

  Need for changes on top
    Levi Strauss examples: S. F. earthquake, Philippine coup
  Qualities required to compete globally
    Flexibility, innovation, empowered work force
  Managing change by unleashing the potential of people

Audiovisual Aids

MAKE IT A JEWEL, LIKE YOUR PRECIOUS EYE.

—*Shakespeare*

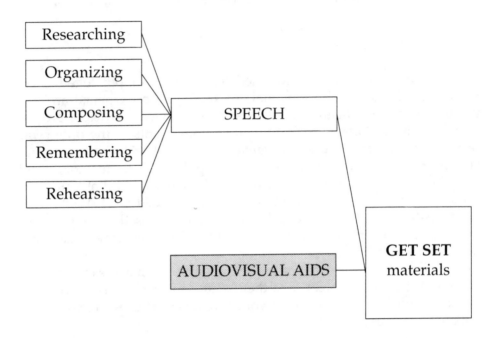

The Uses of the Eye

By nature, human beings are a visual species. Studies show that we pick up information through the eye quicker than any other way. We also retain it up to five times longer.

In the age of television and movies, this natural tendency is reinforced every day. We are trained to pay less attention to what we hear than what we see. In recent years, the stage and even the opera have been turned into visual spectacles, with fabulous sets, spectacular lighting, and grandiose staging taking precedence over the dialogue and even the music.

Using visuals can enhance almost any presentation, making it more exciting. It can also concentrate attention and save time. Rather than reading off facts and figures, which literally "go in one ear and out the other," you can write them out, or provide graphs and charts that express them in an immediate and memorable way.

Which Ones to Use

Different visual aids serve different purposes. Which to use depends on the size of your audience and the nature of what is to be seen. The latest thing is not necessarily the best. It depends on the circumstances.

Presentation Books

Pro: Presentation books are supplied to salesmen or put together by presenters, for use with individuals or small groups. Opened and set up, they become miniature flip charts. They provide a series of professional-quality pictorial aids that illustrate your points in the order you plan to make them. They also summarize and emphasize basic ideas. As you flip from one page to the next, they supply you with memory cues. They look professional and impressive and are economical of time.

Con: Presentation books strongly suggest a canned spiel. While they provide structure, they leave little room for improvisation, responsiveness, or spontaneity. They virtually force both the speaker and listeners through a routine.

Conclusion: Like sales scripts, presentation books make excellent servants but dreadful masters. Use them, but don't let them use you. Be quick to modify your approach if your listeners start showing boredom, impatience or resentment.

Chalkboards

Pro: Sometimes the oldest and most traditional tools are the best. Chalkboards are either permanently installed or are readily portable. They can be used in full light. They are extremely economical and readily erasable. What is on them can be corrected, changed, or replaced. You can write down your points as you go, which lends an air of spontaneity. If you discover a new idea, you can add it and bring it right in. You can also use different colors of chalk for emphasis.

Con: Chalkboards remind people of the classroom. Chalk images, not being illuminated, are not bright enough for groups of over seventy or a hundred. People in back have a hard time seeing what is written low down. Chalk has a way of getting on your hands and clothes and making a mess of you. Writing on the board takes time, and unless you learn to talk while you do it, and keep your face to your audience most of the time, you will lose contact.

Conclusion: Chalkboards are great for relatively intimate, informal occasions, for times when you and your audience will be working out ideas together and making corrections, and under circumstances when you want to keep things simple.

Flip Charts

Pro: Flip charts consist of pads of very large sheets of paper held on easels. As you finish with each sheet, you flip it back over the top of the easel, so as to reveal a fresh surface. They are faster to use than chalkboards, because no erasing is done. They create clearer images because large ink markers of many colors can be used. They can also be employed in well-lighted spaces. They show only one image at a time, yet everything written is preserved on the flipped-over sheets and can be brought back.

Con: Flip charts are usually improvised on the spot, using color markers. Marker colors sometimes bleed through, resulting in a messy look. Some people are sensitive to the fumes from the large markers. Writing takes time, and as with chalkboards, care must be taken not to turn your back on the audience, or you will lose them.

Conclusion: Flip charts are frequently used for internal conferences, because of their speed, vividness, and practicality. They are also good for public presentations where the audience does not exceed sixty to ninety. It's best to limit yourself to messages of no more than a dozen words. Half a dozen would be even better.

Company Flip Charts

Professionally printed flip charts of durable materials are used by sales people and others as part of memorized presentations. These are essentially the same as presentation books.

Slides

Pro: Thirty-five-millimeter color slides provide incomparably brilliant and detailed images. They are ideal for reproducing photographs and fine-line or mechanical drawings, as well as ordinary charts and graphs. They can be used for groups of virtually any size. Because of their high resolution, business and professional slides are best prepared by specialists, using high aesthetic standards.

Con: Slides require a darkened room. Time can be lost in setting things up and making transitions. Audience attention is also distracted from the speaker. Many slides shown in succession tend to blur together and fatigue the audience. Yet it is also tiring to keep repeating the lights-on-lights-off procedure. The order of the slides must be exactly determined in advance, requiring a highly structured and formal presentation. They must also be put into the projector with care, because errors are hard to correct. And you will probably require an assistant to run the projector.

Conclusion: Slides are so troublesome that they should be used only for what slides alone can do. If you are comparing designs for your new headquarters, or demonstrating subtle differences in tissues or fabrics, or showing pictures from your last convention, nothing will do but slides. Even so, structure your presentation so as to limit the total number, the number shown at any one time, and the frequency of the times you have to dim the lights. In between, use a chalkboard, flip chart or some other apparatus.

Overhead Projectors

Pro: Like slides, overhead projectors beam images onto surfaces. They are reasonably portable and can be used in a well-lit room. You can sit or stand facing your audience and glance down into the projector to see the original of the image that is being projected. You can flip the projector off or on from where you are. You can use a pencil or other object to point to the detail you want to emphasize, to adjust the size of the image, and even to cover some parts and then reveal them as you require. You can write or draw additions as you speak, with marking pens of various colors. Projection transparencies can be made quickly and inexpensively, without relying on professionals, by hand-lettering, tracing, freehand drawing, stenciling, or the like. Some projectors provide for the use of dual-spectrum film, permitting you to make transparencies from photographs or printed matter.

Con: Overhead projectors, like slides, tend to separate the speaker from the image, dividing audience focus. The image is less vivid and detailed than those of slides. The equipment is also fairly costly, compared to chalkboards or flip charts.

Conclusion: Overhead projectors are ideal for both semiformal and formal presentations, and for medium-to-large audiences, especially where a quick pace and flexible approach are important and exquisite detail is not required.

Film

Pro: Film is best used to show something in action—how a piece of equipment works, for example. A short strip of silent action will allow you to do your own narration. Sound film is not so much a visual aid as an alternative kind of presentation. It can be shown to audiences of hundreds and even thousands with great impact. People are used to paying concentrated attention to film and associate the whole experience with pleasure. They expect film to be of good quality with attention paid to aesthetics.

Con: Films require elaborate equipment and professional crews to produce. To show, they require yet more equipment and a darkened venue. They are relatively costly to ship and inconvenient to store. Stock films have their own momentum and direction and can distract audiences from the point you want to make. Films tailor-made for your own purposes tend to be prohibitively expensive.

Conclusion: Film is excellent for its own purposes. It is incomparable for portraying action, showing how things work, and conveying a sense of beauty and mood. It is outstanding for surveying a subject and has image resolution on a par with that of slides. But it tends to be inconvenient and impractical.

Videotape

Pro: Videos have become commonplace sales, promotional, and demonstration tools. They cost little to buy, store, ship, or duplicate. Making your own videos is far easier than making your own films, yet they are virtually as effective for demonstrating action and processes. Videos can be played back immediately after being shot, and can be shown in almost any lighting. Audiences are accustomed to watching television screens, feel at home with them, and have learned to forgive a low level of aesthetics.

Con: To show, videos require a VCR, hooked up to a television set or monitor. Video equipment is not readily portable and needs to be available on site. The size of the image is limited by the size of the screen, which in many cases limits the size of the audience. Like films of any length, videos take attention away from the speaker.

Conclusion: Videos are to film what overhead projectors are to slides— less aesthetic but far more practical and therefore preferable for all but the most demanding uses. Like film, they are not so much aids as pre-packaged presentations. Videos shown on standard-sized screens are best suited for intimate audiences. Where supersized screens or multiple monitors are used, there is virtually no limit to audience size.

You on Projection Video

Pro: On certain occasions, your image may be projected onto a huge video monitor as you speak. If you are addressing a very large crowd, this may be necessary. People find it hard to attend to a small, faraway figure. Your projected image will hold their attention much better.

Con: It may feel disconcerting to know that people are not attending to *you* as you speak, but to your image blown up to the size of Lenin's in a pre-perestroika May Day parade. It may bother you that your mouth looks as big as a crocodile's and your nostrils the size of street excavations.

Conclusion: All in all, it's better to be an oversized image than a dot in the landscape. Make the best of it. Inquire in advance what the background colors will be, and dress for quiet harmony and contrast. Don't wear white against white or black against black, or you will look on screen like a disembodied head. But don't go for glittering jewelry or patterned clothing either, as these will undergo prismatic distortion and turn you into a piece of sixties psychedelic art. Remember that the people up front, at least, will be looking at you directly, so make your eye contact with them and ignore all other considerations.

Microphones

Pro: Microphones were the first and are still the most essential of all audiovisual aids. If you have a small voice and a large audience, they are a virtual necessity.

Con: The greatest of all film musicals, *Singing in the Rain,* was made in the 1950s. It portrayed the coming of sound films a quarter century before. Much of the comedy was based on the actors' troubles with the microphones—the voice distortions, the sudden losses of sound, the spills over the cord. Today, we can receive pictures from the planet Jupiter but we are still having microphone trouble. Mikes still distort the voice, tend to break down, and trail perilous cords.

Conclusion: Personally, I do without a mike whenever possible. Most people can learn to project the voice well enough to be heard by any small or medium-sized group. But when a microphone is required or preferred, do be sure to arrive early enough to check out the equipment, and arrange to have a sound person there with you, so the troubles can be handled *before* it's time for your presentation. And watch out for the cord!

Practice

Try to have at least one rehearsal, using whatever A/V equipment you plan to use. If your skills are less than perfect, hone them. If you've never used an overhead projector before, go through the procedure with someone who understands it.

Once you become a highly skilled and confident presenter, you will be able to skip some of these steps. It will be second nature to do things easily and right. You will jump into a presentation the way you jump on a bike, keeping your balance without thinking about it twice.

Checklists for a Perfect Presentation

Dr. George Simons, author of *Men and Women, Partners at Work* and a frequent speaker on the topic of transcultural management, is a firm believer in checklists. He makes sure that checklists of what is needed for a successful preparation go to his clients to help them prepare for the engagement, too.

Dr. Simons insists that if you use checklists for both your speaking materials and your wardrobe from the start, it will enable you to pack the day before the program or departure without frenzied searches. For him, the last 24 hours are critical.

Simons Says
The Last 24 Hours

1. Time your arrival to avoid the extremes of jet lag. Leave time for delays, traffic, etc.

2. Arrive in time to do a final check of the speaking room, preferably the day before for a morning presentation, in the morning for an afternoon or evening presentation.

3. Know how to reach your support person(s) (audiovisual, conference personnel, catering, interpreters, etc.). Meet them personally if possible. Share your objectives and enthusiasm with them. This puts them in your corner and helps them know better what you are doing and enables them to support you.

4. At conferences where the participants are already there, mingle a bit to get the feel and mood of the meeting and to make yourself comfortable with these people. In particular be alert to buzzwords, jargon, or events which may have just happened and which may color their perception of you and your task. Stroll the exhibits if there are any.

5. Do a final preparation—a partial or full rehearsal. When done, reorganize your materials so that they are ready to use.

The Last Four Hours

1. Eat very lightly or not at all. It enables you to feel lean and mean even if you're not.

2. Get some exercise and fresh air, at least a brief walk. It puts your mind back into your body which is, after all, your tool of expression.

3. Leave enough time to preen. Enjoy putting on your costume (and your face). As you do, feel yourself growing into your role and becoming stronger and more influential.

4. In all of this, do *not* rehearse. If you've made a good preparation, the words will be there. Rather, when parts of your presentation come to mind, see and hear yourself doing them well for an instant or two, then let go of them.

The Last Hour

1. Do a quick eyeball check before the participants show up to ensure that your materials (notes, slides, etc.) are in place and that the mechanics of the room (sound system, A/V, etc.) are working.
2. Do a crown-to-soles check of your appearance or have someone check it for you, especially if there's no mirror at hand.
3. Mingle a bit with the participants to get a feel for the mood, especially if you haven't been able to do this the day before.
4. Stop this in time to get focused. Quiet any distractions in your mind. Remind yourself of your purpose and your goals as you breathe deep and feel a powerful energy.
5. Pay attention to your introduction to pick up useful cues to acknowledge the introducer.
6. Be your best self. That's what they are all waiting to hear.

Simons Says
Presenter's Checklist

[ ] Copies of all materials given to participants
[ ] List of all participants, with first and last names, titles, etc.

Preparation of the Meeting Room

[ ] Sound turned off (Muzak, etc.)
[ ] Adequate lighting, shading for the windows if a slide presentation, no glare behind speaker
[ ] Overhead projector/screen, extension cord, extra bulbs
[ ] Flip chart/markers/masking tape
[ ] Black or white board/chalk/markers/erasers
[ ] Table tents or nametags/ashtrays (outside the meeting room)/water and glasses
[ ] Seating arranged according to number of participants and type of function (check with speaker)

For Participants

[ ] List of participants' names
[ ] Meeting schedule/agenda
[ ] Prework and course materials
[ ] Pads or extra notepaper

Chapter Four

Go!

THE SURGEON MUST NOT THINK OF HIS
FEE, BUT THE LIFE BEATING UNDER HIS
HANDS.
   THE ATHLETE MUST IGNORE THE CROWD
AND LET HIS BODY RUN THE RACE FOR
HIM.

    —Ray Bradbury, Zen in the Art of Writing

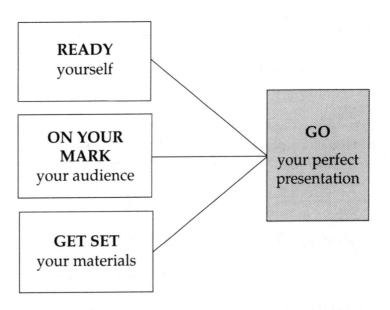

Everything's in place at last. We'll just run through final checks, and you're on.

The Last 24 Seconds—A Visualization Technique

The Hang Glider

You are about to take off. There is an adrenaline thrill coursing through your system that you could call fear or you could call excitement. You would be feeling the same sensations if you were about to go hang gliding. Choose to call it excitement, because that's what it is. So prepare to take off and sail.

Gather Yourself

Remember who you are. Remember that your purpose is to enjoy and to communicate with others.

Breathe

Deeply. Again.

As you do, quickly run through in your mind the opening sentence you have prepared and the outline you have pegged to your memory system.

Imagine soaring easily from one point to the next, using the transitions you have prepared.

Now come to the closing sentence you have memorized. Imagine saying it aloud. Imagine accepting your applause. Imagine your deep breath of relief.

Take that deep breath now.

Eye Contact

Now, go stand in the place where you will speak. Look at your audience. Establish eye contact *before* you say one word. Smile.

Jump Free

Speak the opening sentence you have memorized. Let that be your leap into free flight. Feel yourself taking off, letting your preparation carry you like the wind. Concentrate on what you want to say rather than any particular way of saying it.

Relax and enjoy the moment. It is yours. Know you are about to make *The Perfect Presentation*.

APPENDIX: RESEARCH SOURCE MATERIALS

*T*he following sources are the most frequently used for business-related research. Most will be available in the Reference section of your library, though some will be in the Social Science, Business, or Science and Technology sections.

Multivolume Encyclopedias—General

Encyclopedia Americana
Encyclopedia Britannica
Collier's Encyclopedia
World Book Encyclopedia

Multivolume Encyclopedias—Specialized

Dictionary of American Biography
Dictionary of the History of Ideas
Dictionary of National Biography
Encyclopedia of Associations (Government and Business)
International Encyclopedia of Social Sciences
McGraw Encyclopedia of Science and Technology
New York Public Library Desk Reference
Thomas Register (Manufacturers)

You'll find books on your topic under *Subject* or *Author and Title* in your library's card catalogue. Also try the *Subject Guide* to the reference volume

Books in Print. Any library or bookstore will have a copy. If a book you need is not available locally, you can order it.

The Reader's Guide to Periodical Literature will guide you to articles on your subject in American magazines. It's in the Reference or Periodical section of the library. Articles published abroad are listed in *Ulrich's International Periodicals Directory,* which also provides information on how to send for what you need.

If you need to follow a story on a daily basis, recent newspapers are usually kept in the Reading Room. Older issues are on microfiche. Your librarian will locate the slides for you.

If you need information about federal agencies or congressional committees, try the *Washington Information Directory. The Congressional Record* not only provides all the debates and speeches but gives statistics and committee reports, as well as relevant articles and information from various congressmen. If you need information about state and local agencies, ask your librarian.

Law libraries at universities and law schools tend to restrict access to attorneys and students. But states and many large cities have law libraries open to the public. To inquire, phone the main branch of your public library or City Hall. Some major cities also have dedicated business libraries open to the public. Ask the information service at your main library.

Exploit your main library's phone-in service. If it's something simple, call up and tell them what you want to know. It can save you many a trip. By the way, most libraries now provide photocopying services, so you can duplicate relevant pages and take them home.

If your company subscribes to an electronic fact-finding service, use it. These services provide a wide range of information, from credit reports to preliminary patent searches to historical research. If you don't know how they work, find someone who can show you, or who will be helpful enough to get you the information.